Outstanding resource for anyone who is trying to understa helpful for teenagers who want to know why their parent ha can do about it.

Jeff Pyne, M.D., Psychiatrist. Associate Professor, University of Arkansas for Medical Sciences. Commander and Medical Corps, United States Navy Reserve.

Honest, helpful, direct, therapeutic, and above all, a priceless aid to young people. A MUST for all schools and treatment programs.

Reverend Richard Lutz, Chief Hospital Chaplain, Retired.

Finally—a book that explains PTSD in simple language and guides teens in coping and healing. This useful, sensitive book provides a practical toolbox for the reader. I highly recommend this book for the whole family and for therapists/teachers who are looking for ways to help.

Richard A. Carothers, Ph.D., Psychologist. Chair of the Veterans Affairs Section (Division 18) of the American Psychological Association.

Knowledge is a powerful tool that can limit fear. This compassionate, empowering, one-of-a-kind book will prove invaluable to teens who are struggling to find their way.

Lisa Bekemeyer, M.A., Educator.

This hands-on book is ideal for any teen whose parent has lived through a traumatic life event. The clinical and educational expertise of the mother-daughter Sherman team shines through. Based on well-grounded scientific and clinical knowledge, the book is accessible and welcoming to the reader.

Jennifer Vasterling, Ph.D., Psychologist. Clinical Professor of Psychiatry and Neurology, Tulane University Health Sciences Center. Associate Director for Research of the South Central Mental Illness Research, Education and Clinical Center (MIRECC).

Every day millions of young people experience violence in their homes. This book offers skills to teens in a blame-free, age-appropriate manner. A very important book—the first of its kind. I intend to place copies in all domestic violence programs in Oklahoma.

Marcia Smith, Director, The Oklahoma Coalition Against Domestic Violence and Sexual Assault.

This beautifully written and developmentally appropriate book provides understanding and support to teenagers who are struggling with the results of trauma experienced by their parents. Knowledge can at least partially erase fear. This interactive book gives the reader a chance to vent, to develop insight, and to overcome fear.

Marilyn Coleman, Ph.D., Professor of Human Development and Family Studies, University of Missouri, Columbia.

A very well written, thoughtful manual that will bless the lives of many teenagers. I wish it were already in their hands.

Laura Crites, President, Turning Point Cancer Center. Former Director of Family Peace Center (domestic violence treatment program).

FINALLY! A book designed to empower teens to understand and cope with a traumatized parent. A vital tool for teens, parents, and helping professionals. Speaks to teens in straightforward language and depersonalizes the reasons for their parents' behavior. Most importantly, it helps teens develop coping skills to deal with the aftermath of trauma.

Laura Lochner, Ph.D., Psychologist. Former Chief of the Life Skills Support Center, Head of the Critical Incident Stress Management Team, and Head of the Mental Health Disaster Team at Tinker Air Force Base, Oklahoma.

Devastating events can greatly affect emergency personnel. Families need to know that it is OK to seek help. This book will be a staple not only in my firehouse but in my own home as well...tremendously beneficial.

Stew Shepard, Captain, Apple Valley Fire Department, Minnesota.

Marvelous! Every therapist treating families should have a copy.

Shelli Deskins, Ph.D., Psychologist. Robert C. Byrd Health Sciences Center, West Virginia University.

"Finding My Way" is extremely helpful and enlightening. As a practicing physician, I see great benefit in having my patients give this book to their teens. The book combines academic expertise with skilled writing, making it ideal to read and re-read.

Richard Guiton, M.D., Family Physician. Retired Colonel, United States Army.

Speaks directly to teens, explaining difficult concepts without being patronizing. Does more than just explain PTSD—it helps teens understand and express their feelings.

Laura E. Hankins, J.D., Special Counsel to the Director. Public Defender Service, Washington, DC (personal endorsement).

A great resource for teens whose parents have been touched by trauma! The educational focus de-mystifies and de-stigmatizes the family's experience. The practical, down-to-earth suggestions for coping will be a great help to many youth. Excellent addition to family and professional book collections!

Debora J. Bell-Dolan, Ph.D., Psychologist. University of Missouri, Columbia.

Helps families learn to cope with PTSD and to put skills into practice for more joy-filled lives. Help is in this book.

Rhoda Pfotenhauer, Chaplain and Counselor.

FINDING my WAY

A Teen's Guide to Living with a Parent Who Has Experienced Trauma

Michelle D. Sherman, Ph.D. • DeAnne M. Sherman

This book is intended to provide general information only and is not intended to serve as a substitute for individualized mental health services. If you have concerns about a specific situation, you should contact a healthcare professional directly.

Sunday Night used by permission of HarperCollins Publishers.

ISBN 10: 1-59298-117-8
ISBN 13: 978-1-59298-117-5

Library of Congress Catalog Number: 2005910327

Book design and typesetting: Mori Studio, Inc.
Cover design: Mori Studio, Inc.

Printed in the United States of America

First Printing: December 2005
Second Printing: September 2007
Third Printing: January 2009

12 11 10 09 6 5 4 3

Beaver's Pond Press, Inc.
7104 Ohms Lane, Suite 101
Edina, MN 55439
(952) 829-8818
www.BeaversPondPress.com

To order, visit *www.seedsofhopebooks.com* or call
1-800-901-3480. Special sales discounts available.

Table of Contents

* The Note for Professionals and Note for Parents / Caregivers offer guidance and suggestions on how this book might be used with teenagers.

Foreword

Finding My Way: A Teen's Guide to Living with a Parent Who Has Experienced Trauma is a ground-breaking book that explains the consequences of traumatic stress to teenage children of parents who have been exposed to psychological trauma. Written by Dr. Michelle Sherman, a nationally recognized expert on the impact of psychological problems on families and parent-child relationships, and her mother, DeAnne Sherman, this remarkably sensitive book addresses the confusion and distress experienced by teenagers whose psychological worlds have been inexplicably altered.

This compassionate piece of work helps these teenagers make sense of their changed family environments by providing basic information about post-traumatic stress disorder (PTSD), and by offering gentle suggestions about the use of healthy coping skills. Coping skills that are presented include taking advantage of the healing power of journaling, suggestions about how to communicate with friends about their parents' trauma exposure, and encouragement to talk to trusted adults. The authors provide innovative journal-like sections that allow the readers to normalize their experiences so that they can feel more comfortable with themselves and gain a sense of mastery over their emotionally turbulent family environment.

Families whose teenagers are coping with the realities of trauma exposure should be strongly encouraged to seek help and comfort from this unique text. It could make all of the difference in the world.

Fred Sautter, Ph.D., Psychologist.
Co-chair, Family Studies Team, South Central Mental Illness Research, Education and Clinical Center (MIRECC).
Associate Professor of Psychiatry and Neurology, Tulane University Health Sciences Center.

Welcome

If you have this book in your hand, you may be having some rough times at home with one of your parents. Your mom or dad has experienced a really awful event, and his/her life has changed a lot. Maybe your parent is depressed, and you are **sad** or **frustrated** to see him/her hurting. Maybe your parent has mood swings and seems pretty normal one day, but angry and out of control the next. That can be very **confusing** and **upsetting**. Maybe your mom **embarrasses** you by getting really mad at the referees during your basketball games. Maybe you are **worried** because your dad drinks a lot of alcohol every night and has missed many days of work. You wonder what will happen if he loses his job. Maybe you feel **hopeless** and wonder if things will ever get better. Maybe you are **afraid** that one day you might experience a trauma yourself. On top of all this, you might be really **mad**—asking, "**What is all this about and why is it happening?**"

You're not alone and we're here to help.

In this book, we will:

- Answer questions
- Provide facts and information so you can better understand your parent
- Suggest ways to cope during the tough times
- Help you identify people who can support you
- Give you hope because there are things that you can do to make things better

We hope this guide will help you and your family to find your way.

—Michelle and DeAnne

Before You Begin

We invite you to make this book your own, so write anywhere you wish. Some chapters include questions to consider. If you feel like writing a few words or phrases, go for it. If not, that's OK, too. If you run out of room, use the blank pages at the end of Parts One and Two.

When you answer a question, express your thoughts and feelings in whatever way works for you. There are no right or wrong answers. You may want to write words, phrases, or poems...or even draw pictures.

Another thing about this writing business...don't worry about spelling, grammar, or making complete sentences. This book is just for you. Don't try too hard to get all your thoughts and feelings down perfectly—just start writing and see what comes out. You may surprise yourself with what you find. Sometimes getting it all down on paper can help a lot.

Unlike most books, you don't have to read this book from the first page straight through to the last. You decide which chapters apply to you.

Finally, you may wish to keep this book in a private place. You don't have to share your writing with anyone. Or, you may decide to share parts of your book with a trusted family member, teacher, counselor, or friend. Whatever you decide, remember that it's totally your decision.

As you probably already know, there are few easy answers about trauma reactions, and reading this book may spark some questions. The resource list at the back of the book has websites, phone numbers, and organizations you can contact to learn more. A list of feelings and a glossary of key terms also appear at the end of the book.

Using this book may bring up some tough, unpleasant emotions. That's OK, and we congratulate you for looking inside yourself (because sometimes it's easier to ignore these tricky emotions or pretend nothing is wrong). Dealing directly with your feelings will help you to cope better, both now and in the future. Please remember that feelings are not right or wrong; they just are. Feelings provide you with information about your situation and help you to learn more about yourself.

You will find eight boxes scattered throughout the book that highlight important lessons. Check them out! We also summarize them in Chapter 12.

We hope this book will provide helpful facts, much comfort, and most of all, hope.

And now let's get started!

PART I: The Basics

- What is my parent going through?
- My parent has really changed…what's up?
- Why MY parent? And why NOW?
- Why is my parent so tense and sad?
- Why does my parent turn to alcohol and drugs?
- What can help my parent?

CHAPTER ONE

What is my parent going through? The facts about trauma and PTSD

You may be asking yourself, why should I read this book? What's in it for me? Why did my counselor (or parent, family member, school counselor, teacher, doctor, relative, minister, friend, or other caring person) encourage me to read this book?

The fact that an adult gave you this book means that your family is going through a rough time. One of your parents has experienced a very frightening (traumatic) event that is likely affecting your entire family. Someone obviously cares enough about you to give you this book, and we welcome you.

To get you started thinking, please answer these questions:

HOW ABOUT MY FAMILY?

- ☐ What traumatic experience(s) did your parent have?

- ☐ What is your parent doing differently now than before the trauma? For example, you may notice that your parent sleeps all the time...or doesn't go out of the house much...or gets really angry over little things.

- ☐ How have these changes affected you?

- ☐ How do you feel about these changes in your parent? (You may find it helpful to review the list of feelings at the back of this book.)

Your family life may feel pretty out of control right now. Things may have changed quite a bit since your parent's trauma, and life may feel really different than before. You may feel frustrated that all the attention is going to your parent. You may wonder if other teenagers have ever dealt with these feelings.

Although this book has no quick fixes, our hope is to help you feel more in control of YOU. You obviously cannot change what happened...and you cannot control your parent, brothers, sisters, or other family members...but you do have control over your own thoughts, feelings, and behaviors. You have the power to choose how to respond to the stress in your family, and we want to help you. We will help you feel more in control by giving you:

- Clear information about trauma and its aftermath
- Tools for coping with your feelings
- Encouragement to find and talk to supportive people
- Resources for further learning

> The longer I live, the more I realize the impact
> of attitude on life.
> The remarkable thing is we have a choice every day
> regarding the attitudes we will embrace for that day.
> We cannot change the past...
> we cannot change the fact that people act in
> a certain way.
> The only thing we can do is play on the one thing
> we have, and that is our attitude...
> I am convinced that life is 10% what happens to me
> and 90% how I react to it.
>
> —Charles Swindoll

The Facts About Trauma

It's a sad but true fact that more than half of all people experience a traumatic event during their lifetime. You cannot miss the news bombarding us with stories about terrible events, such as bad car accidents, suicide bombings, hurricanes, child abuse, military combat, and school shootings. Almost every day the media is filled with stories about tragedies that affect people around the world.

Before you throw this book down because it's too depressing, get this: The large majority of people who experience traumatic events go on to lead happy, productive lives. That's good news.

Immediately after experiencing a trauma, almost ALL people have some problems, such as:

- Thinking a lot about what happened
- Feeling nervous or worried
- Having nightmares or difficulty sleeping
- Feeling in a daze
- Finding it hard to concentrate

These reactions are NORMAL.

Thankfully, these problems usually become less intense and often disappear over time. Although the trauma survivors may think about the event once in a while, they have healthy relationships, hold down good jobs, and are satisfied with life. When you think about how awful some traumas are, it's pretty awesome that so many people end up doing really well.

When the Problems Continue

Although most survivors feel much better several weeks after the trauma, some people are haunted by the event for many years. No two people respond to a trauma in exactly the same way. It's almost impossible to predict how a person will cope. Let's consider Jeff's experience of being called to the scene of a very bad car accident.

> Jeff is a volunteer firefighter and has three sons, Scott (17), Chris (15), and Jake (11). One night Jeff's pager went off at midnight and he was called to a terrible car accident. By the time he arrived on the scene, one of the cars had exploded and burst into flames. Although the driver had escaped, two children were trapped in the back seat. The firefighters beat back the flames and rescued the kids, both of whom were severely burned and taken to the emergency room. Because the children were stuck in the car for so long, Jeff worried that they may not survive.
>
> For the firefighters, the ride back to the station was quiet. No one spoke as they took off their gear and prepared to return home.
>
> Jeff's boys had always been proud of their dad's commitment to the fire department, and now they were especially proud of his bravery. They told him, "Dad, you're a hero...just like in the movies!"
>
> But Jeff doesn't feel like a hero. Although it's been six months since the fire, he can't sleep, and he keeps thinking about those two kids, wondering if they survived. He replays the fire call over and over in his mind, asking himself what he could have done differently. He is upset by images of the fire and the smell of smoke that come over him for no clear reason. Whenever he hears about a bad car accident, he shakes uncontrollably.
>
> Jeff's sons don't understand what's going on. Their dad used to be a gentle guy who loved to joke around. Now he stays to himself, mopes around the house, and rarely joins in on family activities.
>
> Scott feels confused and helpless. Although he feels sorry for his dad because he's upset, Scott doesn't understand why and doesn't know

how to help. After all, his dad has worked many fires before—why is this one any different?

Chris is angry—angry that his dad can't put the whole thing behind him, forget about those other kids, and start paying attention to his own family again.

Jake thinks the whole thing is lame. He doesn't understand how anyone can be a hero and be so sad. He wishes his dad would just get back to normal again.

Jeff is experiencing several reactions to his fire call, including some symptoms of post-traumatic stress disorder (PTSD). It is important to remember that not everyone who experiences a traumatic event will develop PTSD. Some people have problems with depression, anxiety, or substance abuse. Regardless of the specific situation, the trauma can affect many aspects of a person's life.

Although the term "post-traumatic stress disorder" is used quite often, many people don't understand what it means. This chapter is dedicated to explaining this concept. PTSD stands for:

Post

Traumatic

Stress

Disorder

Let's begin by looking at each word one at a time.

POST

The word "post" means after-the-fact. Your parent's problems arose after he/she experienced a really upsetting incident. Your parent did not have these difficulties before the distressing situation.

TRAUMATIC (TRAUMA)

A trauma involves experiencing or witnessing a death, a life-threatening event, or a serious injury. The person feels afraid or helpless during the event.

Some common events that may be traumatic include:

- **Military combat**

- **Natural disaster**, such as an earthquake, flood, hurricane, tornado, tsunami, or fire
- **Man-made disaster or terrorism,** such as the World Trade Center attacks, a suicide bombing, or an airplane crash
- **School shooting**
- **Rape or sexual assault**
- **Mugging, kidnapping, or other violent crime**
- **Family violence**
- **Bad car accident**
- **Physical, emotional, and sexual abuse**
- **Torture**
- **Community violence,** such as a riot or gang fight

We usually think about victims of these disasters as people who may develop PTSD. Did you know that people working on rescue and recovery efforts—police officers, fire fighters, Red Cross workers, ministers—can also develop symptoms of PTSD?

STRESS

The word "stress" is used very loosely in our society, and it can refer to feeling worried about a test, frustrated with a traffic jam, or overwhelmed by your "to do" list. The "stress" in PTSD, however, refers to reactions to the trauma.

Traumatic stress can arise in many parts of the survivor's life. For instance, these stress symptoms may arise when the person:

- Has upsetting dreams of the event
- Cannot stop thinking about the event (even though they don't want to think about it)
- Feels distant and disconnected from other people
- Avoids reminders of the event (people, places, and activities related to the trauma)
- Startles easily or is really jumpy
- Has angry outbursts (often for no good reason)

DISORDER

As we explained earlier, it's normal to have some difficulties in the first few days and weeks after the trauma. A mental health "disorder" may be present when the problems don't go away, cause distress, and interfere with daily life (like holding down a job, having good relationships, and socializing with friends).

PTSD can range from mild to serious. The experience of PTSD can be quite different from one person to another. Some people do well for many years, and then hit bottom and go through a rough time. Sometimes the reason for the change is clear, while other times it's a mystery.

So, let's put it all together:

Post	Traumatic (trauma)	Stress	Disorder
happening after the event	a death, life-threatening experience, or serious injury	reactions to the trauma (nightmares, angry outbursts, being jumpy)	problems with thinking and feeling that cause distress and interfere with the person's daily life

Important Points About PTSD

Although some days it may feel like your family is all alone in dealing with PTSD, it can be helpful to know that trauma-related symptoms are actually quite common. Did you know that approximately six to eight percent of people will likely develop PTSD at some time during their lives? To get an idea of what this means, look around your classroom tomorrow at school. If you have about 30 kids in the room, chances are that three classmates also have a parent who has PTSD (or will develop it later). Or, imagine walking down a busy street; 1 of every 12 people you see will develop PTSD at some time during their lives. Remember, you're definitely not alone.

Lesson Number 1

You are not alone!

Although this book is focused on having a parent who has survived a trauma, we know that you may have experienced a frightening event at some time in your life as well. Perhaps nobody knows about the awful thing that happened to you, or maybe your trauma is public and you've already gotten counseling. Regardless of your specific situation, we encourage you to ask for help from a trusted adult (we'll brainstorm specific people in Chapter 9). We also hope that you will find healthy ways of coping with your strong feelings. Check out Chapter 8 for many great ideas. Telling someone about your upsetting event takes a lot of courage and can help you to feel much better. We strongly encourage you to open up to an adult who can support you.

CHAPTER TWO

My parent has really changed... what's up? The symptoms of PTSD

Now that we've reviewed the basics of PTSD, it's time to discuss the specific problems your parent may have. Remember, each person's experience is different—your parent may have all of these symptoms, or just a few. One person may struggle with the problems for many years, while someone else may go for a long time doing well, only to have a crisis appear out of nowhere.

For example:

> Anita and Nadia are next-door neighbors, and both of their homes were destroyed in a terrible tornado. Even though the women had the exact same experience and both of them lost everything in their homes, their reactions are quite different. Anita develops fear of another tornado, has difficulty sleeping, and isolates herself from friends. Nadia, on the other hand, feels sad for losing her special pictures and things in her house, but she focuses on the excitement of getting a new house and does not develop long-term difficulties.

See how different these reactions can be?

Now let's consider two people with the same physical health problem.

> Jimmy and Carlos both have asthma. Jimmy gets short of breath and cannot walk very far without using his inhaler. Carlos has frequent coughing spells and gets allergy shots every week.

Just like Anita and Nadia, Jimmy and Carlos have similar situations but very different responses. As you can see, each person's experience of a physical or mental health problem is unique.

We'd like you to meet a family in which the dad (Greg) experienced combat while serving in the military. As you read about this family, see if you can identify some of Greg's symptoms that could be signs of PTSD.

Greg, a 45-year-old father of two teenagers, joined the military right after high school. After serving stateside for many years, he was called into an intense combat situation overseas and was responsible for a large group of soldiers. In one particularly gruesome battle, Greg made the decision to send some of his troops ahead. He has regretted that decision ever since, as that battle resulted in the death of several soldiers under his command. Because Greg was also wounded in that fight, he received a medical discharge and returned to his hometown.

Greg's sons (Paul, 15 and Doug, 18) were excited to have their dad home again. Greg had been the coach of Paul's soccer team, and Doug hoped that his dad would help build a loft for his dorm room. The boys had really looked forward to hanging out with their dad.

Upon returning home, Greg thought about his combat experiences once in a while, but he kept busy putting in long hours at work. He began using alcohol pretty heavily to help sleep and to take the edge off of his painful memories. Due to his alcohol use, he was unable to perform his duties at work, so eventually he was fired. He also quit coaching Paul's soccer team and stopped working on the loft for Doug's dorm. Greg had other jobs, but lost them because of his bad temper, poor attendance, and coming to work hungover.

Paul and Doug couldn't believe how their dad had changed; they just didn't understand why he couldn't keep a job. The boys had to get part-time jobs to have extra spending money that their dad used to provide.

By the time Greg decides to see a therapist, he has been unemployed for two years and has a lot of time on his hands. Lately he has been having vivid, upsetting dreams about his military buddies, and is waking in cold sweats and shaking. He feels haunted by the decision he made and the soldiers he lost. He gets angry quickly with his wife and family, throws things around the house, and doesn't feel close to anyone anymore. He feels nervous in large groups and cannot tolerate going to busy places like shopping malls. He "just doesn't feel like he's

> the same person" anymore. He often wonders why his good friends were killed but he survived.
>
> Paul and Doug feel robbed and they resent the military for doing this to their dad. Even though their dad is home, he is so dazed and withdrawn that he hardly spends any time with them. They miss the dad they had before he went to war.

Greg has many symptoms of PTSD. Although he was happy before entering the military, the traumatic combat experiences changed his life a great deal. Greg was probably able to avoid facing his feelings about the combat experiences by being a workaholic and by drinking a lot. He is having even more problems now since he lost his job.

The Specific Symptoms of PTSD

There are three major categories of symptoms in PTSD:

- **Re-living the trauma** in various ways
- **Avoiding reminders** of the trauma
- **Feeling tense and on edge** much of the time

Re-living the Trauma

Survivors may **RE-LIVE** (or re-experience) the traumatic event in a variety of ways. People describe feeling haunted by the event because re-living the trauma is pretty upsetting. The re-experiencing can take several forms.

- People may have upsetting **dreams or nightmares** of the event and **intrusive thoughts** during the day (memories or images of the trauma that pop into their minds, often for no clear reason). In fact, over half of people with PTSD experience nightmares. Often, trauma survivors are afraid of going to sleep because they fear having bad dreams. *Remember Greg? He woke up shaking and had cold sweats.*
- Trauma survivors are often upset by **triggers** or reminders of the event. Triggers are places, conversations, and thoughts that are somehow connected to the traumatic event. *If Greg watches a war movie, he might feel anxious, may sweat, and may notice his heart is racing.*

- Sometimes people act or feel as if the trauma was happening again. This experience is called a **flashback**. When having the flashback, the person truly believes that he/she is back in that situation or that it is happening again. Flashbacks are actually rare, but they are very frightening. *If Greg were to have a flashback, he would think he's back in the combat situation. He would see the other soldiers, smell the gunpowder, hear the fire of artillery, and feel the warm sun on his face.*

HOW ABOUT MY FAMILY?

- ❑ Does your parent re-live the trauma? If so, how?

- ❑ How does this affect you? What do you do?

Because it can be upsetting to watch your parent re-live the trauma, it may help you to get away from the situation for a while and talk to a trusted adult or friend. Part Two of this book will describe many helpful ways of dealing with these tough times.

Avoiding Reminders of the Trauma

- Survivors may **avoid thoughts, feelings, places, activities, or people that remind them of the trauma**. Because thinking about the trauma is so painful, survivors may go to great lengths to avoid the memories. Some people change their routines, such as avoiding certain parts of town. Others avoid watching anything on television associated with the trauma, such as war movies or news broadcasts about bombings. Some survivors lose themselves in alcohol or drugs to avoid the memories. (See Chapter 5 for more about addictions.) *Greg worked very long hours and abused alcohol to avoid his painful memories of combat.*

- A trauma survivor may **lose interest in activities** that he/she used to enjoy. The individual senses that "nothing is fun anymore." Trauma survivors can become very isolated from others, with a daily routine of going to work, coming right home, watching television, and going to bed. *Although Greg had enjoyed coaching Paul's soccer team before the war, he quit coaching shortly after getting home.*

- Some survivors **shut down emotionally** to avoid the pain related to the trauma. In doing so, however, they also become numb to other feelings. They may **feel distant from other people** and have a hard time expressing tender or loving feelings. Survivors talk about building "walls" around themselves that protect them from strong emotions and from being close to people. Although the survivor may want to feel close to his/her family, doing so can be difficult and uncomfortable. *Greg didn't feel close to anybody and said that he's just not the "same person anymore."*

HOW ABOUT MY FAMILY?

❑ What does your parent avoid? How does this affect your family?

❑ How does this affect you?

❑ Has your parent lost interest in things he/she used to enjoy? If so, what activities?

- ❑ Have you experienced your parent being distant from you and the family? If so, what has that been like?

Often young people don't understand why their parent stops coming to their activities or no longer talks to them about daily life...or why their parent is zoned out in front of the television or in bed most of the time. It's tempting for young people to wonder if they did something wrong to cause their parent to isolate in this way. As you will soon see, it's not your fault.

Sunday Night

I'm listening to the sounds
of the baseball game
seeping through the wall from the next room

knowing that my father is sitting in there
in the dark
staring at the flickering screen,

too weary to talk
or even to sit in silence
next to someone on the couch.

I'm hating the crack of the bat,
the roar of the fans,
the announcer's stupid voice.

I'm hating these sounds
that remind me
that my dad is in there

with the baseball game,
and I'm in here
alone.

—Sonya Sones (Used by permission of HarperCollins Publishers)

Lesson Number 2

If your parent is distant, it is NOT because he/she doesn't love you.

Your parent may be overwhelmed by strong feelings and bad memories.

If you look closely, you'll probably see that your parent is not only cut off from you, but is cut off from just about everyone and everything. Therefore, remember: It's NOT ABOUT YOU (even though that may be hard to remember when you feel hurt and sad). We encourage you to talk to people you can trust about these feelings. In Part Two, we will give you ideas of people who may be able to help you.

Feeling Tense and On Edge

Because the survivor feels uptight and restless much of the time, it's very tough to relax. Little daily hassles can produce strong emotional reactions (often anger). The survivor's strong feelings make it hard to do everyday activities like grocery shopping, paying the bills, and getting along with other people.

- Due to trauma survivors' chronic nervousness, many have **insomnia** (problems falling or staying asleep) and get very little rest at night. Memories of the trauma may make it hard to fall asleep; bad dreams may wake them up and prevent them from falling back to sleep. If you've ever had problems sleeping, you know that this is really frustrating! Furthermore, you're often crabby and cannot concentrate the next day. *Greg's poor sleep kept him from making it to work on time every day.*

- Many people with PTSD have problems with their temper and have **angry outbursts**. It's pretty easy to understand why trauma survivors feel angry—after all, we all feel angry when we are threatened or hurt, when we feel out of control or taken advantage of, or when life isn't fair. However, some trauma survivors get stuck in their anger for a long time and may be crabby and blow everything out of proportion. People with PTSD tell us their anger feels very strong and it gets intense very quickly. *Greg often got angry with his wife and children and threw things around the house—his family never knew when he would "go off."*

- Some survivors pay a lot of attention to what is going on around them. Because trauma often involves feeling out of control, survivors want to be **very sure of their surroundings**. Although awareness of the environment is understandable when you're in danger, such as on the front lines in combat, many traumatic events happen when and where you would least expect it—bombings that harm people in schools, churches, homes, and workplaces. Therefore, some survivors cannot let go of this extreme need to focus on their surroundings…even when in a safe place. Some people become preoccupied with potential danger lurking nearby.

Survivors may sit with their backs to the wall in public places (like restaurants) to be aware of all that is happening around them. If someone does approach unexpectedly, the survivor may be quite **startled** and jumpy. Because being around a lot of people feels out of control, survivors often avoid social situations. *Greg disliked large groups and busy shopping malls.*

HOW ABOUT MY FAMILY?

Which of the following words describe your parent's anger or temper? Check all that apply.

- ❑ Furious
- ❑ Out of control
- ❑ Rage
- ❑ Steaming
- ❑ Scary
- ❑ Hard to predict
- ❑ Unfair
- ❑ Taken out on the wrong person
- ❑ Violent
- ❑ Out of the blue
- ❑ Hurtful
- ❑ Quick
- ❑ The silent treatment
- ❑ Mean
- ❑ Other: ____________________
- ❑ Other: ____________________

Dealing with your parent's anger is such an important issue that we're going to spend extra time on this topic.

Some days your parent may seem really mad—for NO GOOD REASON! He/she may yell at you when you didn't do anything wrong. Sometimes your parent may even swear at you or call you names. You may worry about what will set your parent off. You may try to be extra good to prevent an angry outburst. It may feel like you just can't win—no matter what you do, your parent seems really mad. If your parent has unpredictable bursts of anger, you may feel on edge and scared, always wondering when your parent will flare up again.

Most of the time your parent's anger has nothing to do with you. Although your parent may be upset by the memory of the traumatic event, his/her angry feelings may get taken out on you since you're the closest person around. It may be hard to remember that you didn't do anything wrong, especially if you're the one getting yelled at. Although your parent may not be feeling well, having PTSD does **not** excuse unkind behavior. Regardless of your parent's mental health, it's never OK to hurt a child, emotionally or physically. If your parent acts in a mean way, your job is to **steer clear** as much as possible and to take care of yourself. Calling a friend, reading a book, or going for a run may help you to feel better. Part Two of this book will suggest many good ways of taking care of yourself during the difficult times.

Complete the following sentences:

- ❑ I feel really scared when my parent…

- ❑ When this happens, I know that it's best for me to…

Most people with PTSD are no more dangerous than anybody else. However, there are times when survivors may threaten others or act in a violent way. If you **ever** feel in danger, leave the situation immediately and contact a trusted adult. If necessary, call 911 for help.

- ❑ Three people I can call at any time for help are (please list their names and phone numbers here):

____

____

____

Now that we've reviewed some key points about your parent's anger, let's look at other ways in which your parent's tension and nervousness may affect your family.

Sometimes people with PTSD need to be very sure of their surroundings and may do unusual things in public. For example, some people may get really jittery at loud noises such as firecrackers or planes overhead. Others may act as if the traumatic event is occurring again and get really focused on their surroundings. For example, your dad may frequently check the perimeter of the house, believing danger is nearby. Your mom may install several deadbolt and chain locks on every door of your house, and check the locks several times every night. Some people with PTSD become loud and angry; they may have road rage or get into fights. These situations can be embarrassing and scary for the family.

Think about a time when your parent acted in an embarrassing way in public. Describe it. Where were you? What was happening?

❑ What was that situation like for YOU?

❑ How did you cope with it? What did you do?

This chapter covered a lot of important information, including the key symptoms of PTSD. We hope you recognized some of your parent's problems in this chapter, and that you remember that you are not alone. The next chapter answers three common questions that teens have about PTSD. Part Two of this book describes helpful ways of dealing with your feelings when your family situation feels out of control.

Want to learn more about PTSD?

Check out Chapter 14 for a list of websites and other books.

CHAPTER THREE

Why MY parent? And why NOW? Risk factors for developing PTSD

Many teens have questions about their parent's difficulties. Even knowing the textbook definition of PTSD doesn't explain everything, and family life can be pretty confusing. Consider the poem below, written by the 14-year-old daughter of a veteran who served in the Vietnam War. Her dad had many symptoms of PTSD. Can you relate to her questions and feelings?

Tell Me Daddy, Please Why

Tell me Daddy, please why?
Is it because you have seen friends die?
Is it because we're poor?
Please Daddy, I need to know more.
Is it because you know you can do more than you do?
Is it because you had to kill people you never knew?
Do you suffer extreme guilt?
Guilt that has made your hopes wilt?
Daddy, Daddy, can you ever quit?
Could you make it bit by bit?
Don't you know that it hurts when you get on the phone
And my friends hear that nasty, drunken tone?
Can't you get help from me?
Is there anything I can do to make you see?

I'm not a child any longer.
Can I help to make you stronger?
Or must I always see you cry?
And always be until we die?

—Jennifer Miller
circa 1986
Daughter of Gene and Marsha Miller

This chapter takes a look at three questions that many kids have about PTSD. You may feel uncomfortable asking the questions, but they're actually very important...and you deserve to know the facts.

QUESTION ONE

Why did MY parent develop problems? After all, many people have experienced traumatic events, but not everybody has PTSD.

GREAT question! In fact, scientists are working hard even now to try to answer this question...but we don't yet fully know.

We do know that the chances of developing problems after a trauma are affected by three key issues:

- **The kind of trauma**
- **The individual's personality and past experiences**
- **What happened after the trauma**

Typically, it's a combination of these three issues that determines if an individual will have problems. Yet, it is impossible to predict how a specific person will respond to trauma.

The Kind of Trauma:

What was my parent's trauma like?

And, how involved was he/she in the trauma?

People are more likely to develop PTSD if:

- **They were very close to and personally involved with the trauma.**
  - Firefighters who rescue people from burning buildings and people involved in serious car accidents are at higher risk for having problems because they are closely involved in the trauma.
- **They were exposed to traumatic events for a long period of time.**
  - People who survive years of abuse or who were on the front lines of combat for many months may be at higher risk of developing PTSD than people who had one upsetting incident.
- **The trauma was impossible to predict.**
  - The several hundred people who entered the Alfred P. Murrah Federal Building in Oklahoma City on April 19, 1995 thought they would have a regular workday. They could never have predicted that a terrorist would set off a bomb that would kill 168 people.
- **They feel responsible for the trauma or feel betrayed by someone they know.**
  - Many people who have been sexually abused by ministers feel betrayed by the clergyperson, and sometimes by the church in general. People abused by a relative may feel betrayed by the family. Being abused by someone you know and trust brings up different feelings than being abused by a stranger.

The Individual's Personality and Past Experiences:

How was my parent doing before the event happened?

The individual's life experiences and personality are related to the chances of developing symptoms of PTSD. For example, if the survivor had depression or anxiety before the trauma, he/she would be at higher risk for having problems afterward. People who experience more than one traumatic event are also more likely to have problems. For example, consider Lisa's situation:

> In tenth grade, Lisa witnessed a shooting in her high school. Although several of her friends were badly hurt, she was not injured. She had nightmares for the first few weeks after the shooting, but thought about it less and less as time went on. After graduating from high school, she joined the military and was

assigned to a very dangerous combat zone. Many fellow soldiers died during her tour. If Lisa develops some PTSD symptoms, her problems may be due to an interaction between her traumatic experiences. Her distress about the military casualties may remind her of the shooting at her high school.

What Happened After the Trauma:

What happened in my parent's life after the traumatic event?

The chances of having problems resulting from a trauma sometimes depend on what happens after the event. Survivors who have a lot of supportive people in their lives are less likely to develop PTSD. Having support from family and friends helps the survivor to reconnect with others, to feel less alone, and to feel loved. On the other hand, survivors who don't get support or who face people who blame them for the trauma are more likely to have later difficulties. For example, some soldiers returning from the Vietnam War were taunted and called "baby killers" by opponents of the war. Instead of enjoying "welcome home" celebrations and parades, these veterans were criticized and blamed. These veterans not only struggled with their awful combat experiences, but they also felt hurt by many people in their hometowns.

Also, survivors who have good coping skills tend to do better. Knowing how to get through rough times and how to deal with strong emotions decreases the chances of developing PTSD. Let us introduce you to two adults, Lakeisha and Steve:

Lakeisha and Steve were both in serious car accidents. They both had long hospital stays, followed by months of painful physical therapy.

During their recoveries:

Lakeisha lifted weights to release stress, attended church to maintain her spiritual strength, and volunteered at the community blood drives.

Steve, on the other hand, stopped all his previous activities and became isolated; he drank a lot of alcohol and smoked marijuana to numb himself from painful memories and feelings.

Because Lakeisha used many positive coping tools, she may be less likely than Steve to develop problems later.

QUESTION TWO

My parent seemed to be fine for a long time after the trauma—why is he/she having such a hard time now? I just don't get it.

This is another important question. Sometimes survivors appear to be leading a "normal" life for many years, only to fall apart later for no clear reason. Family members and friends can feel confused because of the sudden change.

Although symptoms of PTSD usually emerge within three to six months of the trauma, some individuals do not start having problems until much later. Some people avoid facing the painful emotions and memories for many years; they may do this by busying themselves with work or family life, or by getting lost in addictions like alcohol or drugs. For example, many survivors become workaholics, spending 80–100 hours per week on the job, which distracts them from the bad memories. However, when the person no longer has that distraction, the memories and feelings may return. It's quite common for survivors to start having problems when they retire or when their children leave home. Now that the survivor has more time on his/her hands, it's harder to avoid the bad memories, so some PTSD symptoms may appear.

Another reason for PTSD symptoms to surface could be hearing about or experiencing another trauma. Destiny, a rape survivor, may see a movie that depicts sexual assault. Seeing this movie may cause her to remember her experience, raising many painful feelings that she has tried to avoid. Marques lost his house and several good friends in an earthquake five years ago. When he watches the news today describing other earthquakes, strong emotions could bubble up inside. Again, family or friends may feel confused as to why Destiny and Marques are having difficulty now, but the problems make a lot of sense when you understand the triggers.

QUESTION THREE

Why can't my parent just forget about the trauma and move on with his/her life? It happened so long ago...why is my parent still upset about it?

Going through a life-threatening experience can change your life forever, so it's impossible to just "forget about the past." You would never tell someone with cancer to just "get over it," and PTSD is no different. Survivors tell us that hearing this kind of advice from others is very hurtful, because these comments show that others don't understand their experience and their pain. Although treatment can help the survivor cope with the memories and enjoy close relationships, most survivors don't forget about what happened.

Lesson Number 3

People with PTSD can't "get over it" just like that.

Although this chapter has answered three common questions, we bet that there are other things that are confusing for you.

? What other questions do you have about what your parent is going through?

___

___

___

Who could you talk to about these issues?

___

___

___

Remember: You may want to check out the websites and books listed in Chapter 14 to get some answers, too!

CHAPTER FOUR

Why is my parent so tense and sad?

Anxiety and depression

Although PTSD is one reaction to trauma, there are actually many different ways people respond to traumatic events. This chapter will explain three specific challenges faced by trauma survivors:

- **Panic attacks**
- **Social anxiety**
- **Depression**

You may have recognized your parent's behavior in the lists of PTSD symptoms in the last few chapters. Or, you may find that the conditions reviewed in this chapter better describe your parent. It's also possible you will see your parent dealing with more than one problem, since people with PTSD have an increased risk of having several mental health difficulties.

Because living through trauma can be painful, it makes sense that your parent may feel anxious and depressed. After all, survivors often replay the traumatic event over and over in their minds—that can be hard to deal with. Parents who have experienced trauma often feel badly that they are too nervous to attend their kids' games or music concerts. These parents know that they are hard to get along with and are frustrated that their anger is out of control.

Please remember that every person is unique. It's impossible to predict how a specific person will respond to trauma.

Panic Attacks

A panic attack (or anxiety attack) involves suddenly feeling extremely afraid or uncomfortable. The person has several of the following symptoms:

- Racing or pounding heart
- Sweating, chills, or hot flashes
- Trembling or shaking
- Feeling short of breath
- Chest pain
- Feeling of choking
- Upset stomach
- Dizziness or feeling light-headed
- Feeling afraid of losing control, going crazy, or dying
- Numbness or tingling sensation

Panic attacks are VERY frightening and usually last about ten minutes. Some people have attacks several times a day, while others may have them a few times per month. Sometimes the person can identify what set off the attack, while at other times it seems to come "out of the blue." People never know when an attack may come on. Therefore, individuals are worried about when they may have a panic attack. Sometimes people become isolated and rarely leave their homes for fear of having an attack in a public situation.

Many trauma survivors experience panic attacks. The attack may result from being exposed to a reminder of the trauma—or the panic attack may seem to come from nowhere.

Let's meet Bill to learn how trauma survivors may be affected by panic.

Bill is a 44-year-old who was in a serious motorcycle accident. He spent three months in the hospital, followed by six months at home in a full-body cast. Now Bill is back at work, but he is never sure what will set off some strange feelings.

Often when he is in traffic, sees another motorcycle, or smells gasoline, he begins to sweat and his whole body shakes. He becomes dizzy and feels like he might throw up. He fears he may be having a heart attack, or maybe even going crazy. He is always worried that he may be in a situation where having another episode would be really embarrassing.

After surviving a traumatic motorcycle accident, Bill is experiencing panic attacks.

HOW ABOUT MY FAMILY?

- ❑ Has your parent ever had a panic attack? If so, what happened?

- ❑ What was the experience like for you? How did you feel?

Family members often don't know how to help their loved one during a panic attack. You may feel helpless and worried. You certainly cannot prevent your parent from having a panic attack, and you cannot make it stop. Your parent may appreciate your help in getting to a quiet, calm place and getting adult assistance if needed.

- ❑ What is most helpful for your parent while he/she is having an attack? (If you're not sure, ask your mom/dad during a calm time.)

- ❑ Has your parent withdrawn from others due to these panic attacks? If so, how?

Want to learn more about panic attacks?
Check out the specific resources listed in Chapter 14.

Social Anxiety

Social anxiety (also known as social phobia) is the fear of being in a social or performance situation in which you may be watched closely or evaluated. The person is afraid of feeling embarrassed in front of others. Therefore, the person tries to avoid the situation at all cost. If the person must be in the situation, he/she feels very anxious and may experience a panic attack. About one in ten people experience social anxiety that gets in the way of their daily lives.

Many people who have survived trauma also experience social anxiety. Let's consider Juan's situation.

> Juan, a father of two, was a stockbroker in the World Trade Center when it was attacked on September 11, 2001. He was on his way to a meeting when the plane hit the building. Flying glass, fire, smoke, and panic surrounded him. Eventually he made his way safely out of the building, but he has never been the same emotionally.
>
> His experience in the World Trade Center caused him to have many symptoms of PTSD. Because he feels self-conscious, he avoids being in public. He is afraid that people will judge him, or that he might say or do something to embarrass himself. His son resents that Juan doesn't attend his debate team competitions, and his daughter wishes her dad would go to her track meets. His wife misses going out to fancy restaurants with her husband, but she understands that he fears others will see his shaky hands and restlessness.

While Juan was fortunate to survive the attack on the World Trade Center, his personal life has really changed. His social anxiety affects his ability to work and socialize.

HOW ABOUT MY FAMILY?

- ❑ Does your parent experience social anxiety? If so, how?

- ❑ How has your mom/dad's social anxiety affected your family?

Want to learn more about anxiety disorders?
Check out the helpful resources in Chapter 14.

Depression

Everybody has days when they feel tired, down, and bored with life. That is normal. "Major depression" is different. It is a serious illness involving deep sadness and a lack of interest in fun activities that lasts for several weeks. When depressed, people find it hard to follow a daily routine of going to school or work, doing household chores, and interacting with other people.

Depression is very common. Did you know that 17 percent of adults experience major depression? Approximately **14 million** people in the United States deal with depression every year. Depression is about twice as common in women as in men.

A person experiencing depression may:

- Feel very sad or down
- Lose interest in activities that they used to enjoy
- Lose their appetite or feel hungry all the time
- Feel tired and sleep a lot (or not be able to sleep well)

- Struggle to concentrate and make decisions
- Think about death

Among individuals who have PTSD, almost half of them will also go through major depression.

Let's consider Stephanie's situation to learn how trauma survivors may experience depression.

> Stephanie is in an abusive relationship with her husband, Brad. They have been married for 15 years. Brad has beaten Stephanie so badly that she has gone to the emergency room several times. He also tells her how "dumb" and "ugly" she is. She has started to wonder if he may be right.
>
> For the past month, Stephanie has almost completely shut down. She rarely sees her kids off to school in the morning, and is usually still in her pajamas watching television or sleeping when they get home each afternoon. The kids hate seeing their mom cry all the time and wish she would do things with the family more often.

Due to the severe abuse, Stephanie is experiencing many symptoms of major depression.

HOW ABOUT MY FAMILY?

❑ When my parent is depressed, he/she...

❑ When my parent stays in bed all day, I...

- ❑ When I see my parent cry a lot, I feel...

- ❑ When my parent is crabby for days on end, I...

What helps you cope when your parent is going through a depressed time?

See Part Two of this book for suggestions on how to cope and care for yourself when your parent is depressed.

NOTE:

Sometimes people feel guilty for having survived a trauma when others were killed or severely injured. The survivor wonders, "Why did I make it out of that awful situation when others didn't? After all, I'm no different than they are...right?" Questions like these can haunt people and can worsen feelings of depression and anxiety. This is called "survivor guilt."

Want to learn more about depression?
Check out the helpful resources in Chapter 14.

CHAPTER FIVE

Why does my parent turn to alcohol and drugs?

Common addictions among trauma survivors

As you've seen in the first four chapters, people who experience trauma go through a wide range of painful thoughts and feelings. Some survivors use excellent coping skills. They may draw upon close friends and family for support. Others may participate in counseling or take prescribed medications. Some survivors use spiritual or religious support to get through the rough times. Many people exercise regularly to release stress.

However, some people behave in ways that are confusing to others. They are trying to numb the pain, avoid memories of the event, and decrease feelings of emptiness and nervousness.

These survivors are desperate for something—oftentimes anything—to ease their pain and make the upsetting feelings go away. Sometimes survivors develop various addictions. Also, as we'll see later in this chapter, other people think about death or suicide in an effort to escape their painful feelings.

Addictions

First, let's talk a little bit about the term "addiction." We say someone is addicted when he/she becomes obsessed with getting something specific, often with little care about the consequences of their actions. The person's life may become consumed with getting the "fix," and he/she may become anxious when the desired item or activity is not available. Often the person loses him/herself in the addiction, hoping to run away from other problems in life. For example, someone in a troubled marriage may work 80 hours per week and take frequent business trips to avoid an unhappy relationship. Further, an addict may need more and more of the substance over time. For example, a gambling addict may be satisfied with $200 a night at the casino at first, but later may need $500 per night to feel satisfied.

Although we most commonly think of people being addicted to drugs and alcohol, individuals can actually become addicted to a variety of things. For example, people sometimes become addicted to:

- The Internet
- Shopping
- Gambling
- Prescribed medications such as pain pills
- Sexual activities
- Overeating
- Physical exercise
- Pornography
- Work

These addictions share the goal of temporarily escaping reality. The addiction provides a short-term fix or distraction from the challenges of everyday life.

Addictions are quite common in America today. For example, about one in six Americans abuses alcohol or street drugs at some point in their lives. We know that people with PTSD are even more likely to abuse alcohol and other drugs. There is a 50-75 percent chance that a person with PTSD will abuse alcohol at some time during his/her life. Similarly, there is a 25-35 percent chance that he/she will abuse street drugs.

Why do you think that many trauma survivors abuse alcohol or street drugs?

____

____

____

How might alcohol and drug abuse create even more problems for these people?

____

____

____

Does your parent use alcohol or other drugs to self-medicate or numb him/herself? If so, how does that affect you?

____

____

____

Let's consider Debby's situation to understand the answers to these important questions.

> Debby is the mother of two teenage daughters, Heather and Amy. She is a nurse who has volunteered with the American Red Cross for the past ten years. After the tsunami in 2004, she traveled to Southeast Asia for three weeks. Although she was an experienced volunteer, nothing prepared her for what she would see in Indonesia. Heather and Amy had always been proud of their mom for her work with the Red Cross. They knew she would really help the survivors of the tsunami.
>
> Debby spent four weeks in Indonesia providing medical care, serving meals, and reuniting families separated by the tsunami. Being a parent herself, seeing these scared, sad children and the desperate parents was extremely upsetting. While performing these duties, she frequently saw the remains (body parts) of people killed in the disaster. She also saw parents carrying their dead children.
>
> Heather and Amy kept in touch with their mom by e-mail and could tell that she was seeing some awful things. They were anxious for their mom to come home. Heather needed help with her cheerleading fundraiser and Amy was looking at colleges for next year. Besides, they just missed their mom.
>
> Although Debby was able to perform her duties quite well while in Indonesia, she started having difficulties right after returning home. She had bad nightmares of dead children; she would wake up sweating, crying, and feeling very scared. She tried to talk to her husband about her dreams, but he had a hard time understanding her. She also isolated herself from her friends. Her family noticed that she was crabby and cried almost every day; she seemed to be "in her own world" most of the time.
>
> Heather and Amy could not understand what had happened to their mom and they wondered when she'd be back to normal. Both girls were confused by their mom's behavior and felt pretty angry that she wasn't supporting their activities.

> Since Debby felt so anxious, depressed, and cut off from everyone, she started drinking alcohol. At first, she would have just a few drinks at bedtime to help her sleep and to forget about her experiences in Indonesia. However, in a matter of several weeks she drank more and more heavily…to the point that she was drinking a 12-pack of beer daily. Just last week, she was arrested and got a DUI (driving under the influence) while she was driving Heather to cheerleading practice.
>
> This last episode was more than Heather and Amy could handle. They were afraid to have friends over to the house because their mom may be drunk, and the DUI was really awful. They were angry, embarrassed, and fed up.

Why did Debby turn to alcohol? If we asked her, she would likely give four reasons.

- **Trying to relax:**

  "I'm just so edgy all the time. I need the alcohol to relax!"

As we discussed in previous chapters, trauma survivors often feel irritable and anxious. They may feel nervous much of the time. If you can think of times when you've felt restless (such as before giving a speech, before a big game, or before a big test at school), then you know that this isn't a very good feeling. For you, the nervous feeling usually goes away shortly after the event. However, for people with PTSD, this anxious feeling may be around much of the time. So, some people with PTSD use alcohol or drugs to relax. Debby may believe that using alcohol is the only way that she can get through the day. Drinking alcohol or using drugs may help people to feel calm, but only for a little while.

- **Trying to sleep:**

  "You know I can't sleep…I need a few drinks to help me doze off."

Debby is using alcohol to help her fall asleep. While alcohol can help people fall asleep, it actually worsens their ability to get a good night's rest. Using a lot of alcohol can also result in feeling hungover, irritable, and tired the next morning. These unpleasant feelings make people think they need more alcohol to feel better, thereby creating a vicious cycle.

- **Trying to forget:**

  "I drink to forget."

Debby was afraid that her family would not understand her experiences in Southeast Asia, so she usually kept her memories to herself. However, these bad feelings churned inside of her, causing upsetting nightmares. Some trauma survivors, such as Debby, abuse alcohol in an effort to avoid memories of the trauma.

Remember that one of the three categories of problems in PTSD involves avoiding reminders of the trauma. Survivors avoid places, conversations, and people that remind them of the trauma. Abusing alcohol or drugs actually deepens the survivor's avoidance because the substance numbs the person to his/her feelings and memories. Although the survivor may be relieved to be distracted from the immediate painful memories, the problems remain when the effects of the alcohol/drugs wear off.

- **Trying to escape:**

  "I drink to escape my depression—I just need something to help me feel better."

Sensing that no one could understand her experiences, Debby kept everything to herself and became very sad. Alcohol does NOT make depression disappear. In fact, alcohol acts as a depressant. That is, alcohol actually makes people more depressed.

As you can see, Debby had a lot of reasons she turned to alcohol. She was probably coping the best that she could at the time. However, she had already gotten arrested for driving while under the influence, and more problems are ahead if she continues abusing alcohol. People who abuse alcohol or drugs often have many short- and long-term problems:

- **Difficulties on the job** such as being hungover, calling in sick, poor work performance, and an inability to get along with the boss and co-workers
- **Financial problems** such as spending a lot of money on the addiction, getting fired from a job, and not paying bills on time
- **Relationship problems** such as frequent arguments, emotional distance, affairs, and even divorce

- **Physical health problems** such as the direct physical harm on the body caused by the alcohol and drugs and the indirect harm such as poor eating habits
- **Legal problems** such as being arrested, appearing in court, spending time in prison or jail, and enduring probation or parole

So, how can these trauma survivors be helped?

As you will see in the next chapter, there are many different kinds of treatment for trauma survivors. **The challenge for individuals with PTSD is to learn healthy coping skills so that the alcohol and other drugs are not needed.** Obviously, this task takes a lot of work for the entire family. Survivors cannot get as much out of counseling, and prescribed medications don't work well if the person is using substances.

Survivors who also have addiction problems need treatment from a professional who is specially trained in both trauma and addictions. Treatment works best when both issues are addressed at the same time. The survivor may attend 12-step groups such as Alcoholics Anonymous (AA) to help stay off alcohol and drugs. Because the survivor is no longer covering up the PTSD symptoms with alcohol or drugs, the problems related to the trauma may actually become more intense for a while. However, a sober survivor is much more ready and able to deal directly with these issues in counseling.

You and your family may benefit from talking to other families who are struggling with addictions. Just as AA exists for the person with the addiction, there are support groups for spouses, children, and other family members of addicts. Perhaps you have heard of Al-Anon, a 12-step program for adults who are affected by a loved one's alcohol problem. Have you ever heard of Alateen? This is the 12-step program for teenagers whose family member abuses alcohol or drugs. Alateen provides free, confidential support groups across the country where you can to talk to other teenagers in similar situations.

He stares with those eyes full of pain
The ones he tries to hide with alcohol...
...He sits and sleeps, fading everything away
Like his life means nothing but drinking.
He acts like we're nothing to him
I know deep inside somewhere, my dad is there.

—James (from Alateen)

To learn more about Alateen and to find meetings near you, check out the following resources: www.al-anon.alateen.org or 1-888-4AL-ANON. Meeting other teens will remind you that you are not alone and will show you how other people are coping with the same challenges that you face.

Suicidal Thoughts and Behaviors

Some trauma survivors are in so much emotional pain that they want to escape their situation altogether. Perhaps survivors have become isolated and cut off from any support and feel alone in the world. Some people don't know how to stop the memories and think suicide is the only way to make the pain disappear. They may not want to die or leave you—they just want the pain to stop. Of course, thoughts about suicide are very scary and need to be taken seriously.

Why do trauma survivors think about suicide or harm themselves?

People who have experienced traumatic events—especially combat, rape, domestic violence, and sexual abuse—and people who have PTSD are at greater risk for suicide. Although each person's situation is unique, a few risk factors have been found:

- As we discussed in Chapter 4, many people who have PTSD also experience depression and depressed people are more likely to think about suicide.
- Because substance abuse impairs judgment and worsens depression, trauma survivors who abuse alcohol or drugs are at higher risk for suicidal thoughts.
- If you put depression and substance abuse together, the risk for suicide is even higher.
- Sometimes people with PTSD don't know how to let other people know how badly they are hurting. These individuals may not really want to die—but they talk about suicide or attempt suicide as a "cry for help." However, because you don't know if they're serious or not, it's important to take *all* comments about suicide seriously.

Although we can sometimes figure out why a person thinks about suicide, many times there is no clear reason for the person to try to end his/her life.

What should I do if my parent talks about suicide?

Find a trusted adult and tell him/her right away! Hearing your parent talk about wanting to die can be very scary and confusing...and you probably wouldn't know what to do. Your parent may ask you to promise not to tell anyone. Even if you make this promise, it's important that you tell a trusted adult. It's better to break your promise and help keep your parent alive than to keep the secret and risk your parent hurting him/herself!

If you're not sure who to talk to, you can always call a suicide hotline. The national phone number is: **1-800-SUICIDE (1-800-784-2433).**

You can also find a local suicide hotline by looking in the front of any phonebook. When you call, a hotline worker will listen to you, ask questions, and help you deal with this tough situation.

If you think your parent is in immediate danger and no adults are around, call **911** immediately. Again, your parent may become angry with you in the short run, but it's important to get your parent help right away. Also, your parent will probably thank you later for getting the much-needed help.

CHAPTER SIX

What can help my parent? My parent's treatment plan

Great progress has been made in understanding and treating trauma survivors. A lot of research is being conducted right now, and new medications and treatments are always being developed.

Personalized treatment plans—a plan created specifically for your parent that often includes counseling and medications—can help people get back to enjoying their lives. Living with PTSD is similar to living with a chronic physical health problem such as asthma or diabetes. Scientists have yet to discover cures for these diseases. However, with a proper diagnosis, a healthy lifestyle, and regular medications, people living with asthma, diabetes, and other chronic illnesses can enjoy a rich and full life.

So, of all the available treatments...what can help my parent? Treatment for people with PTSD often involves several elements, including:

- **Therapy (or counseling)**
- **Medications**
- **Support groups**
- **Family involvement**

Lesson Number 4

A lot of help is available for your parent.

People typically do best when they participate in several of these kinds of treatment. Let's look at them one at a time.

Therapy

Therapy gives your parent a chance to talk about his/her feelings and experiences. Many different kinds of professionals provide counseling, including psychologists, social workers, marriage and family therapists, and ministers. Therapists with special training in helping survivors listen carefully to your parent's concerns and provide support. In counseling, your parent may learn helpful skills for coping with problems. Hopefully your parent feels comfortable talking to the therapist about his/her feelings and finds that person to be caring and helpful. The therapist may also encourage your parent to write about the traumatic event as a way of coping with painful feelings. Counseling is not magic and cannot make problems go away, but it can help your parent cope with the problems.

Several forms of therapy exist:

Individual Therapy: Your parent meets alone with the therapist, often for 45-60 minutes at a time, to discuss personal concerns.

Group Therapy: Your parent meets with other trauma survivors and a therapist, often for 60-90 minutes at a time, to discuss concerns common to all group members. Talking to other people who have gone through a similar experience can be very reassuring for trauma survivors. They learn that they are not alone! That's a great feeling for your parent.

Couples or Family Therapy: Both of your parents—and perhaps you, too—attend sessions with a therapist to discuss how PTSD affects your family and how all of you can cope with the challenges.

Regardless of the format, therapy for trauma survivors usually involves working on the following issues:

- Learning how to deal with strong feelings such as anger, shame, depression, fear, and guilt
- Learning how to cope with memories and reminders without feeling overwhelmed
- Discovering ways to relax
- Getting back to doing fun activities again
- Improving relationships with family and friends

Being in therapy is HARD WORK. Although having someone listen while you talk about your problems may sound easy, it actually can be pretty difficult because you're discussing painful issues. Remember that one of the key issues in PTSD is avoidance. Trauma survivors avoid places, people, and conversations that remind them of the trauma. Individuals with PTSD often spend a lot of energy staying away from the bad memories.

If you think about it, participating in therapy is the opposite of avoidance—therapy involves confronting the feelings and memories directly. So, it's important to remember that it takes a great deal of courage to go to therapy. It's quite common for trauma survivors to wait several years before starting counseling, thinking they'll "get over it."

> Courage doesn't always roar. Sometimes it is the quiet voice at the end of the day saying, "I will try again tomorrow."
>
> —Anonymous

Now that you understand what therapy involves, hopefully you can encourage your parent to stick with therapy...even when it's tough. You may want to tell your parent how proud you are of him/her for doing this hard work. Remember that counseling won't erase your parent's problems, but can help a lot in coping with the issues every day. Therapy can help your parent get back to being the kind of person he/she was before the trauma.

Medication

Your parent may take medications to help his/her symptoms. Mental health medications are often prescribed by psychiatrists, who are medical doctors who specialize in treating emotional problems. Although medications cannot cure PTSD or make your parent's problems disappear, the depression and anxiety can become less intense. Medications can help your parent to do better in everyday life.

It's important to understand that most of these prescribed medications are very safe and are NOT addictive. Your parent won't get hooked on them. Drugs used to treat PTSD are different from illegal street drugs, such as cocaine or heroin, which can be dangerous. Prescribed medications improve the way the brain works so that your parent feels better.

Some medications have side effects, but usually people get used to them or switch to a different medication. The side effects may also go away with time. Your parent needs to talk regularly with the doctor to find a good plan of medications for his/her needs. Remember this good news: Many medications are available, and your parent's doctor will select the best drug(s) for your parent's specific concerns.

Support Groups

Support groups exist for many different issues and can help your parent feel less alone. Support groups are similar to group therapy (described above), but most support groups are led not by a therapist but by people dealing with the same problem. For example, Alcoholics Anonymous or "AA" helps people with alcohol or drug addictions. The Depression and Bipolar Support Alliance supports people battling depression, and Freedom from Fear helps people struggling with anxiety. Your parent can learn a great deal by talking to others who are dealing with similar problems. Your parent can also help others by sharing his/her experiences and coping skills.

Family Involvement

Family participation in treatment is really important. Families are sometimes confused and not sure what to do. Family members may read books, search the Internet, attend counseling, and attend support groups. Getting involved in your parent's treatment shows that you care, and it can help your family get along better.

Lesson Number 5

Family support is important.

As we already mentioned, some people participate in couples or family therapy. This can be a great approach for helping families deal with many difficult challenges. Other family members may attend workshops or support groups just for the family members. By being involved in your parent's treatment, you can learn about PTSD, figure out what to do when your parent is having a rough time, and focus on taking good care of yourself.

Managing Crises

Sometimes people go through really tough times and need more support than is available from regular doctor visits and support groups. For example, your parent's symptoms may get worse and he/she may be unable to keep up the daily routine of taking a shower, going to work, and sleeping regularly. Your parent may think seriously about suicide or may use dangerous amounts of alcohol or street drugs. When these crises arise, a brief stay in the hospital can be helpful in getting your parent stabilized.

During hospital stays, your parent gets close, personal attention from many professionals, including doctors, therapists, nurses, and social workers. The doctor may change your parent's medications to help him/her feel better. Your parent may have individual, group, or family therapy to learn how to cope better with problems. Usually hospital stays are quite short, and the doctor tries to get your parent home as soon as possible.

In summary, people with PTSD who participate in counseling, take their medications, draw upon family support, get help when crises arise, and take care of their bodies (by getting enough sleep, eating a balanced diet, and exercising regularly) often lead happy, productive, meaningful lives.

A Final Important Note of Hope

Although most of this book is focused on the problems your parent may be facing since the trauma, we want to highlight some good news. Scientists have discovered that some trauma survivors experience POSITIVE changes after the event. Have you ever thought about that?

Sometimes living through a trauma teaches people that they have a lot of inner strength. People may get in touch with courage that they never knew they had. Some survivors grow spiritually. Other people recognize how fragile life really is. They may re-evaluate their priorities, often taking time to appreciate and love the important people in their lives. Some survivors say that surviving the trauma helped them refocus their lives, and they are grateful for the chance for a fresh start at life.

HOW ABOUT MY FAMILY?

Think about your parent for a minute:

- ❑ Have you noticed any positive changes since the trauma? If so, what have you seen?

- ❑ Have you told your parent that you've noticed these nice changes? (He/she would probably really like hearing that from you!)

Please use these pages for any additional thoughts and feelings that surface as you use this book.

You may wish to answer some of the questions more than once.

You may decide to draw something or write poetry to describe your feelings.

Whatever you decide, this space is for you.

PART II:
Life with a Parent Who Has Experienced Trauma

- Are all of my feelings normal?
- How can I cope with all of this?
- Who can I count on?
- What do I tell other people?
- What can I do to help?

CHAPTER SEVEN

Are all of my feelings normal? Understanding my strong emotions

Being a teenager can be a lot of fun, but it can also be a difficult time. Your parents may be giving you more freedom and independence as you get older. You may have more responsibility than you did when you were younger. You may notice your emotions have grown stronger than when you were a child.

Your anger feels more intense.

Your happiness feels greater.

Your sadness feels awful.

Feelings can be very powerful. All of your feelings matter and are OK. It's helpful to pay attention to how you feel and to have a safe place to share your thoughts and emotions. We hope you consider expressing your feelings in this book or talking with a trusted adult or friend.

Some days you may worry about your mom or dad. The next day you may feel hopeful because your parent is having a good day and seems back to his/her "old self." Other days you may feel really mad at your parent. It's normal to experience all of these feelings. You may also feel several emotions all at once. For example, if your dad doesn't make it to your soccer game, you may feel both mad and hurt. You were really hoping that he would come to cheer you on, but you also understand how difficult it is for him to be in large crowds.

Lesson Number 6

It's normal to have a wide range of feelings about your family.

Sorting through your mixed feelings can be tricky. In fact, you may find yourself having a hard time concentrating on schoolwork because you're worried about your family. Your grades may be dropping, you may be getting in trouble at school, or you may be having conflict with your friends. With all that you are juggling right now, it's understandable that you may struggle to manage these important parts of your own life.

Just being a young person these days is tough enough…much less adding the extra issues involved in having a parent who has experienced trauma. We hope that learning more about your parent's situation will help you feel more in control of your life.

Let's take a look at some common feelings young people experience. We will discuss how to handle these emotions in the next chapter.

Confusion

Having a parent with PTSD can be pretty confusing. By working through this book, you will know more about PTSD than most adults. Teenagers living in this family situation may wonder why their parent developed PTSD and when their parent will be back to "normal." Kids may feel confused about why so much of the family attention goes to their parent's day-to-day welfare, and wonder why the family doesn't pay more attention to the teen's activities and needs. Sometimes teenagers find it hard to know who to talk to—or even what questions to ask.

Complete the following sentences:

- ❑ I feel really confused when my parent…

❏ I wish someone would explain…

❏ Sometimes I wonder if my parent will ever…

❏ I really don't understand why…

Lots of stuff still doesn't make sense!

❏ Questions I'd like to ask MY PARENT who experienced trauma:

❏ Questions I'd like to ask ANOTHER FAMILY MEMBER:

- ❑ Questions I'd like to ask A DOCTOR:

____

____

____

- ❑ Questions I'd like to ask A TRUSTED TEACHER, ADULT FRIEND, OR MINISTER:

____

____

____

Anger

Living with someone with PTSD can be unpredictable. Your parent may not be able to be there when you'd like. Your mom or dad may do things that cause you to feel mad or frustrated. Although our society teaches us that it's not OK to be angry, we totally disagree. Anger is a basic human emotion that can give you important information. It's how you choose to act on that anger, not the feeling itself, that can be tricky. Poor choices can have negative consequences, which is why anger sometimes gets a bad reputation. In any case, it's normal to feel angry at your parent and your family situation. Accepting your parent and feeling compassion for his/her struggles may take time.

Think about a time when you felt really mad. Describe it.

What were you thinking?

What did you do?

Sometimes I feel really angry. I hate it when ____________________ (list three things that really upset you):

1. ____________________
____
____

2. ____________________
____
____

3. ____________________
____
____

Sometimes kids feel angry toward a variety of people. For example, some young people feel:

angry at *my family* because *I just want to hang out with my friends and live my own life without having to worry about all these family problems*.

angry at *my parent* because *I don't know why he/she has to be like this. I feel deserted and abandoned at a time that I really need my mom or dad to be there for me*.

angry at *my friends* because *they have perfect lives and don't have to deal with all this garbage*.

angry at *God* because *I don't know why He did this to my parent*.

Think about who you are angry at and why:

I'm angry at ______________ for causing this to happen to my parent.

I'm angry at ______________ for / because ____________________

____ .

I'm angry at ______________ for / because ____________________

____ .

How could you tell these people how you feel?

Hint: When you choose to say tough things, it's helpful to focus on your own feelings and avoid blaming the other person. One way of doing this is called an "I message." The format looks like this:

"When you *(describe the person's specific behavior that upset you)*,

I feel or felt *(identify your specific emotions)*."

For example, Paul (from Chapter 2) may express his anger to his dad for abusing alcohol and for quitting coaching Paul's soccer team by saying:

"Dad, when you *quit coaching my soccer team and started drinking all the time*, I felt *angry and hurt*."

Amy (from Chapter 5) might express her disappointment to her mom for failing to help explore different colleges by saying:

"Mom, when you *wouldn't help me fill out the college applications and think through my choices*, I felt *lost and unloved*."

What do you want to say to your parent?

"Mom / Dad, when you ________________________________

I felt ________________________."

Shame

At times you may feel ashamed of your parent. You may feel embarrassed by your mom or dad's behavior. You may avoid having friends over to your house because you don't know what kind of mood your parent will be in. You may feel badly when your friends' parents attend the homecoming football game or dance recital, but your parents don't show up even though they said they would. These feelings make a lot of sense when your parent's behavior is so unpredictable.

Think about a time when you felt ashamed or embarrassed about your parent's behavior. Please describe it. What did your parent do or say?

What was most difficult for you in that situation?

What were you thinking?

What did you do?

Some kids feel ashamed for even feeling ashamed or angry. This can be pretty confusing. For example, consider how 15-year-old Ramon felt in the following situation:

> Ramon was angry with his dad for missing his choir concert. Ramon had a special solo in the concert. He was disappointed when his father gave the excuse of "I'm too tired." At first Ramon couldn't believe his dad was going to miss this important concert. However, later Ramon felt badly about himself. He thought, "I really shouldn't feel angry with my dad. He's going through a lot right now and doesn't sleep well. Maybe I don't have a right to feel angry at all."

Of course Ramon had every right to feel angry with his dad. It's common to question yourself about your emotions, but please remember that feelings are not right or wrong. All feelings are OK. If you judge yourself for your emotions or deny how you honestly feel, you will probably end up feeling even worse. We encourage you to pay attention to all of your emotions, see what you can learn from them, and then use the coping strategies described in the next chapter to feel better.

Sadness

Caring about someone who has experienced trauma can be very tough. You may feel sad that your parent has gone through such a terrible event, and you wonder if he/she will ever be normal again. You may feel hurt that your parent doesn't come to your school activities anymore. You may let others know that you are sad, or you may keep these feelings to yourself. (We encourage you to talk to a trusted adult, however, if your sadness is really strong or lasts for several weeks...or if you have thoughts of suicide.) Please know that it's normal to feel sad. **It doesn't mean you're going to feel sad forever.**

Think about a time when you felt really sad. Describe it.

What were you thinking?

What did you do?

> There will be dark days...but they will not last forever.
>
> The light will always return to chase away the darkness,
>
> the sun will always come out again after the rain,
>
> and the human spirit will always rise above...
>
> —Rabbi Harold S. Kushner

Complete the following sentences:

- ❑ Some days I wish I could just wave a magic wand and my parent would be all better. When I see my parent struggle for a long time, I feel...

- ❑ Some days I want to cry and to be left alone. When I feel this way, I want my family to know...

- ❑ During the tough times, it can be helpful to remember that my parent loves me by:

  Looking at ____

  Maybe pictures of fun times?

  A gift your parent gave you?

  Remembering ____

  What the doctor told you?

  That your parent still loves you?

  Talking to ____

  Who could you talk to?

  What else? ____

Fear

Fear is a powerful emotion that can include feeling frightened, scared, nervous, or worried. All human beings live with a certain amount of fear, and fear can help us make good choices, such as not walking down a dark alley at night or speeding excessively when driving.

In families in which a parent has experienced trauma, young people may wonder if the world is a safe place. For example, you may feel nervous riding in a car because your mom was in a serious car accident. Although this fear is understandable, it's important to remember that millions of people drive cars every day and very few people have accidents. Although it's terrible that your parent experienced a traumatic event, please remember that most tragedies are rare.

Your parent may talk a lot about *staying safe* because he/she lived through a very frightening experience. He/she may frequently check the locks on the doors, keep loaded guns in the house, or put lots of security lights around the house. Although these acts may comfort your parent, they may lead you to feel nervous and afraid. You may also feel scared if your parent acts out his/her anger in frightening ways.

Although you may not talk about your fears a lot, you probably face some scary issues. Below we list some fears other kids have expressed about their family situations.

Check the statements that you can identify with:

- ❑ I get scared when my parent is out of control. I don't know what he/she might do.
- ❑ I worry that my parent may never be normal again.
- ❑ I'm afraid of sharing my feelings because people might ignore me or make fun of me.
- ❑ I worry about what other people think about our family.
- ❑ I worry that my family will depend on me too much and that I will never be free to live my own life.
- ❑ I'm afraid that I might experience a trauma someday, too—or maybe even develop PTSD myself.
- ❑ I wonder what will happen in the future.

What other fears can you identify?

As a kid, focusing too much on these fears and worries can interfere with your daily routine. Therefore, be sure to read the next chapter that reviews many helpful ways of coping with your fears.

What helps you to feel safe when you are afraid? Where do you go? What do you do?

NOTE:

Remember:

As difficult as these feelings may be to recognize and experience, they are all normal and OK!

What Other Emotions Do You Feel?

Now that we have reviewed the five common emotions of confusion, anger, shame, sadness, and fear, let's consider some other feelings you may be having. Teenagers experience a lot of different feelings, and each person's emotional world is unique. Please try to avoid judging your feelings. Accepting all of your emotions helps you to move through the difficult times.

Circle as many as apply to you and write in others that come to mind. A list of feelings is included near the back of this book.

Bored	Hopeful	Proud
Curious	Hurt	Really down
Depressed	Important	Resentful
Different	Invisible	Strong
Forgotten	Left out	Understood
Frustrated	Lonely	Worried
Guilty	Numb	___________

Think about a time when you felt one of these emotions strongly. Describe it:

How did you cope with that situation? What did you do?

Sometimes we feel numb or sense we're not feeling anything at all. This can be confusing when we think we "should" be upset about our family challenges. We may keep ourselves busy and distracted so we don't have to think about what's going on. We may have convinced ourselves that our family situation hasn't affected us at all.

However, you may notice that you're getting sick a lot. Your frequent headaches and stomachaches may be trying to tell you something. Or, you may be getting into trouble at school or arguing with your friends and siblings. Sometimes your behavior can serve as a warning sign that you really do have some uncomfortable feelings about your family situation. Working with a trusted adult to identify and deal with these feelings can help you feel more in control.

Activity

Your feelings are so important. They tell you a lot about yourself and how you're doing. If you like creative projects, you might enjoy this activity. Turn on a computer and find a draw and paint program (it's called "Paint" in some programs). Create a collage of all the feelings you are experiencing at this time. You may use different colors, shapes, textures, words...anything you want. If you don't have easy access to a computer, you can also cut pictures out of magazines. Just be creative and see what happens!

What do you notice about your collage?

Does this picture express how you feel?

Sometimes you may be having a really tough day, but you don't want other people to know. Let's consider how Avery deals with this situation:

> Avery is worried because his mom hasn't slept in several days and she is acting strangely. Avery wants to ignore the mess at home, but actually feels very worried. He tries to act normally at school and around his friends. This works OK for a while, but eventually things feel out of control and it's just too tough to pretend anymore. He talks to his school counselor, and feels better when she listens and offers helpful tips.

Popular psychology uses the term "wearing a mask" to describe faking how you really feel. Wearing a mask can usually work for a little while. However, if you get in the habit of hiding your feelings, you may become lonely and feel even worse. Feelings stuffed inside can give you other problems, such as headaches, stomachaches, or difficulty concentrating. Therefore, it's important to find a safe, healthy way to express your true feelings.

Can you think of a time when you wore a mask? If so, what happened?

...What did your mask *say?*

...What did your mask *hide?*

> The only feelings that do not heal are the ones you hide.
>
> —Henri Nouwen

Is there anyone in your life or any place you can go where you don't need a mask?

Activity

One way of sorting through strong feelings is by writing your parent a letter. After you finish, you decide whether or not to give it to your parent. Sometimes writing a letter and then ripping it up can feel really good and help you understand your emotions.

Just start writing and see what happens. If you need help, you could start off using some of these prompts:

Mom/Dad:

- ❑ I really want you to know that...
- ❑ I thank you for...
- ❑ I want you to understand that...
- ❑ I admire you for...
- ❑ I miss how our relationship used to be. I miss (share the things you used to do together—or describe how it used to be)...
- ❑ When you ________________, I feel ________________.
- ❑ I wish that we could (share how you'd like your relationship to be now or what you'd like to do together)...

____

____

____

____

____

____

____

____

____

CHAPTER EIGHT

How can I cope with all of this? Tools for getting through the rough times

As we've discussed throughout this book, dealing with a parent who has survived a trauma can bring up many strong feelings. This chapter will focus on some very important issues such as:

How can I sort through all of my emotions?

What can I do when my feelings are really strong?

What should I do when life feels out of control?

There are many things you can do when you are worried, down, or angry. Some kids cope by using alcohol or street drugs, behaving in dangerous ways, or hanging out with the wrong kinds of friends. These choices not only prevent you from facing your family situation head-on, but can also create major, long-term problems. Healthy coping tools can help you feel better both now and in the long run.

Let's start off by considering the following activities, known as coping tools, which have worked for other young people. Rate each activity on a scale of 1-5 according to how helpful it is (or might be) for you.

1	2	3	4	5
Not at all helpful		Kind of helpful		Very helpful

______ Hang out with friends
______ Shoot hoops
______ Watch TV or a movie
______ Surf the Internet
______ Lift weights
______ Pray or meditate
______ Write in a journal
______ Call a friend
______ Exercise
______ Listen to music
______ Take a shower
______ Volunteer or help someone
______ Play with your pet
______ Talk to a counselor or minister
______ Read about PTSD
______ Cry
______ Go to a peaceful place to relax
______ Play videogames
______ Take deep breaths
______ Take a nap
______ Send a text message or e-mail
______ Read a book or magazine
______ Go to the gym
______ Play a musical instrument
______ Go for a walk
______ What else? ________________

You may have never tried some of these coping tools. What works for one person may not work for someone else—so be sure to consider several options. **Circle two tools** that sound interesting to you and try them this week. See how they work.

As you can see, there are lots of different ways of dealing with strong emotions. How you choose to cope depends on a lot of things including how you feel, who is around, and what you need at the time. There's no such thing as a perfect coping tool—and remember, anything taken to extreme can cause problems.

Lesson Number 7

Remember to take good care of yourself and have your own activities.

Let's consider five teenagers and how they cope with their feelings and family situations.

Carmen

Carmen feels really confused about her mom's PTSD. She doesn't understand why her mom does the grocery shopping late at night and why she is anxious during Sunday church services. She also doesn't get why her mom won't let her have friends over to the house.

One Good Way to Cope: Gathering Information

When we feel puzzled, it can be reassuring to face the situation head on, approach it logically, and learn more about the topic. Gathering facts and getting "into our heads" can help us understand the situation and feel less afraid. Knowledge is powerful.

For example, Carmen finds it helpful to:

- Surf the Internet for information about PTSD and anxiety
- Ask her mom in a gentle way why being around large groups of people is so uncomfortable
- Read a book
- Talk to her dad about why her mom avoids crowds
- Ask her psychologist, doctor, or school counselor

Once Carmen understands that her mom's discomfort in large groups is related to having been mugged nine months ago, Carmen feels less confused and frustrated. She and her mom come up with a plan in which Carmen can have just one or two friends over to the house instead of a large group.

Where could you get helpful information about PTSD?

Nathan

Nathan has had it with his family. He is stressed by all the chaos in his house and thinks about his family problems all the time. He hates how his dad, who has PTSD, yells a lot and gets mad over little things. Nathan needs a break!

One Good Way to Cope: Distracting Yourself and Having Fun

When we feel overwhelmed by life, it can be a great release to kick back and have fun. Sometimes it's healthy to forget about your family problems and enjoy yourself. Although it's not a good idea to avoid reality all the time, taking a break once in a while is very important.

When Nathan wants to escape the stress at home, he likes to:

- Listen to his iPod
- Play videogames
- Read a book
- Hang out with his friends
- Watch his favorite movie
- Surf the Internet

After doing these activities, Nathan can put his family problems into perspective and is better able to deal with them.

Did you know that preschool children laugh an average of 400 times per day?

QUESTION: Guess how many times per day (on average) that an adult laughs?

ANSWER: 15

What works best for you to distract yourself from your family's stress?

What makes you laugh and have fun?

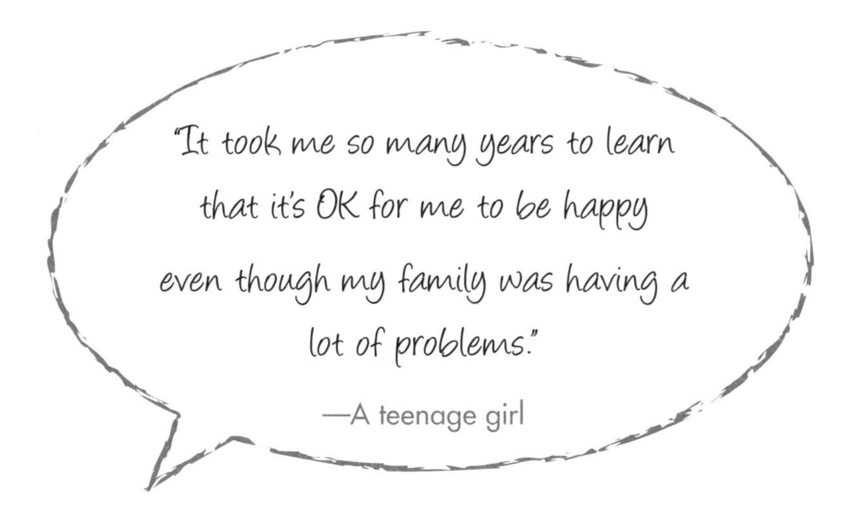

Angela

Angela feels really alone in dealing with her family situation. She is a quiet person and doesn't feel like anyone understands how her family is affected by her dad's difficulties. Ever since getting back from the war, her dad hasn't been the same person. She wonders why her dad is so withdrawn. She'd love to find a way to let her feelings out.

One Good Way to Cope: Expressing Your Feelings and Finding Support

When we have lots of emotions bubbling inside, it can help to find a way to express our feelings. Just putting a name to your feeling can begin the process of coping. (The list of feelings at the back of the book can help you to identify how you feel.) Some days you may share your feelings with someone else, while other times you want to get the feelings out on paper. Regardless of how you do it, you'll probably feel better after having let some of those emotions out!

Angela finds that it really helps her to:

- Journal in her diary
- Talk to her best friend
- Draw or create a picture on the Paint program on her computer
- Write poems or short stories
- Talk to and pray with her youth minister at church

Angela learns that she feels a lot better after expressing her feelings because she doesn't have to hold everything inside anymore.

How can you directly express your feelings?

Who can you talk openly to about your feelings?

Hannah

Hannah isn't quite sure exactly what she's feeling, but she knows she's stressed about her family's situation. Her stomach is often in knots and she gets headaches a lot. She feels tired much of the time. She worries about her mom, a police officer, who has been depressed ever since witnessing the fatal shooting of a fellow officer in the line of duty. Hannah would give anything just to relax.

One Good Way to Cope: Relaxing

When we feel tense and worried, we often experience the stress in our bodies. This mind-body connection is clear in Hannah's situation because she gets headaches and stomachaches when stressed. When we are worked up, it can help to do something that calms us. Hannah learned some tools in counseling that help her feel more peaceful.

Hannah finds peace by remembering to:

- Take deep breaths
- Take a shower
- Do yoga or pilates
- Imagine walking along a beautiful beach and feeling the warm sun on her face
- Play the piano
- Remind herself that she's strong and will get through this tough time
- Say prayers before going to sleep
- Play with her dog, Buddy

As Hannah practices these new behaviors, she notices that she has fewer stomachaches and sleeps better.

What can you do to calm your spirit?

Is there a special place that is peaceful for you?
(In your house? At a church / place of worship? In nature?)

Richard

Richard, whose dad has PTSD from a car accident, gets so worked up that he feels he's going to burst. Richard is fed up with his dad's behavior, and has started talking back to his parents and teachers. Richard feels tense all the time and doesn't know what to do with all the pent-up feelings and energy. He really needs to blow off some steam.

One Good Way to Cope: Doing Something Physical

When we need to release stress, doing something physical can be just the answer. Get up, go outside, and do something. Not only does physical activity feel good at the time, exercise actually releases chemicals in your brain that give you energy and help you to feel better.

Richard knows that it helps him to:

- Lift weights at the gym
- Go for a run
- Play pick-up basketball
- Go on a bike ride
- Skateboard

Since spending more time at these activities, Richard feels less stressed and has made some new friends.

What physical activity helps you to release stress?

In summary, we've reviewed five good ways of coping with strong feelings:

- Gathering information
- Distracting yourself and having fun
- Expressing your feelings and seeking support
- Relaxing
- Doing something physical

One More Coping Tool to Consider: Helping Others

Through living with a parent with PTSD, you have probably learned a great deal. One way for you to cope can be helping other kids who are in similar situations. You could be very helpful to another young person whose parent has PTSD. It would also feel good for you to make a difference in another teen's life by sharing your experiences.

If you met another teenager in a similar situation, what would you be sure to tell them? What would be important for them to know?

____

____

____

____

____

____

____

____

____

____

____

____

____

CHAPTER NINE

Who can I count on?

Identifying people who can support me

Kids often feel alone in dealing with PTSD in the family, and they feel like no one understands. You may have chosen to keep the situation to yourself, or you may have confided in a few friends. Whatever you have decided, it's good to know who you can count on—no matter what.

Finding out who you can go to for support is an important first job. We hope you select people who will do their best to:

- Listen to you without interrupting
- Encourage you
- Respect where you are without judging
- Keep your conversations private

In this chapter we will focus on two groups of people who may be able to support you, namely your family and people in your community.

My Family

People in your family can be great resources. They probably know more about your family situation than your friends do, and may like the chance to talk to you about it.

When we refer to your family, we're not just talking about the individuals who live in your house. Family can include:

Parent
Stepparent
Brother
Sister
Aunt
Uncle
Cousin
Grandparent
Godparent
Good friend of the family
Anyone else?

All of these people may be able to support you. Let's think about these individuals:

- ❑ Even if my parent is having a rough day, I know I can count on some people in my family. The person who understands me the best is (please write the person's name and phone number below):

  ____

- ❑ The family member who makes me laugh when I'm sad is:

  ____

- ❑ The family member who will listen when I need to talk is:

  ____

- ❑ If I want someone to be there when I need to cry, I know I can count on:

  ____

- ❑ The one thing I'd like my family to understand about my feelings is:

  ____

Other People in My Community

Some family members are great, but you may want to get help from people outside your family as well. You may worry that your brothers and sisters or your other parent are too stressed themselves to really be able to listen to you. Or, they may be too close to the situation to be objective. So, let's look at your social world.

To identify your social world, we'll create a map.

1. You are in the middle, so write **your name** in the middle circle.

   You see the two circles outside the one with your name in it. Let's call them the "inner circle" and the "outer circle."

2. In the **"inner circle"** write the names of all of the people you trust and feel close to today. These people could be of any age. They could live nearby or across the country. You could see them every day or just once in a while. None of those factors matter. What's important is that you feel comfortable with them and see them as trustworthy.

   Consider these people for your circles:

friends	school counselors
neighbors	ministers
teachers	coaches
dance teachers	youth group leaders
a friend's parent	

3. In the **"outer circle"** write the names of people you know pretty well, but don't know if you can trust them or not. You believe these people care about you, and you *may* decide to open up to them in the future.

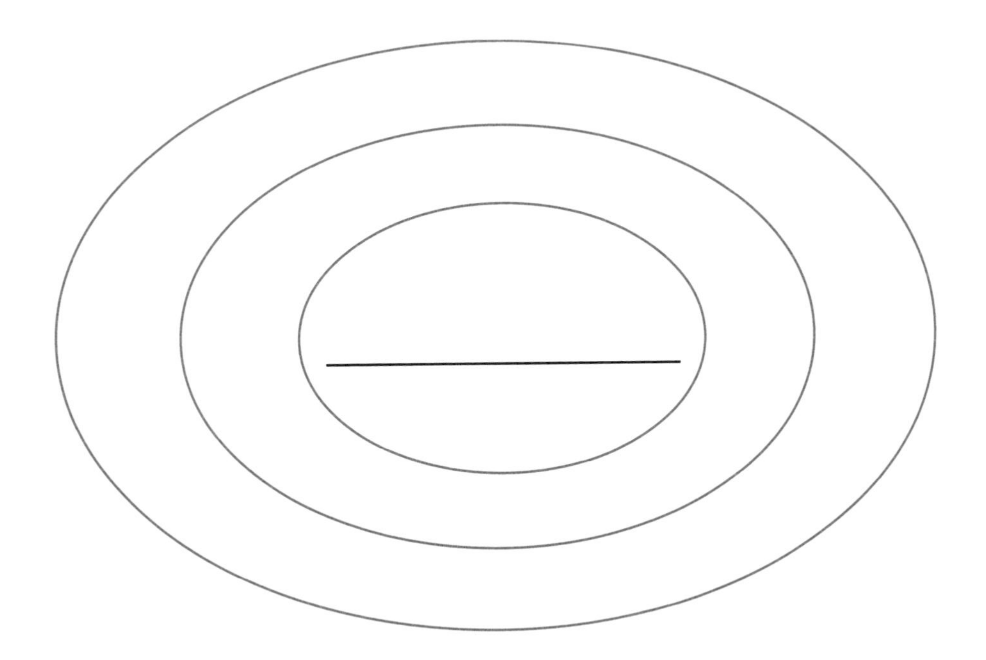

What did you notice in mapping your support network?

Might there be other people you'd like to add to your group? Think about three people you would like to join your circle. List their names here:

1. ______________________________

2. ______________________________

3. ______________________________

Depending on how you feel and what you need, you may select different people in your support network at different times. For example:

- ❑ Some kids feel comfortable talking to people at school. Teachers, principals and school counselors can be helpful and can listen well. Someone I know I could count on at school is (please write the person's name and phone number below):

  ____

- ❑ Someone I can talk to at any time of the night or day is:

  ____

- ❑ An adult I can talk to if I feel in danger and need to be protected is:

  ____

- ❑ A place I can go if I feel in danger is:

  ____

- ❑ The person who helps me keep my sense of humor is:

  ____

- ❑ When I'm really mad, the best person to talk to is:

  ____

- ❑ The person in my support network who understands me the best is:

  ____

- ❑ The person who I know FOR SURE will not tell others what I tell them (unless someone is in danger) is:

  ____

"In the beginning of life, when we are infants, we need others to survive, right?

And at the end of life, when you get like me, you need others to survive, right?"

His voice dropped to a whisper.

"But here's the secret: in between, we need others as well."

—Mitch Albom quoting his aging mentor, Morrie Schwartz, in *Tuesdays with Morrie*

CHAPTER TEN

What do I tell other people? Dealing with my friends

Most kids want to fit in, feel normal, and be like other kids. Everybody wants to be accepted and liked by friends—but this can be especially important during the teenage years.

Sometimes young people feel insecure when they sense that they don't fit in. For example, they may fear other kids won't like them if they don't wear the right kind of clothes, are not a great athlete, or don't live in the right neighborhood. Sometimes you have control over these things, but many things are probably out of your control. Having a parent with PTSD is one of those things you simply cannot control or change...and this can be tough.

You've probably heard other kids express anger about their parents, so you know that feeling frustrated with your family is common. After all, no family is perfect! Every family has its own unique difficulties, such as physical health problems, divorce, money problems, alcohol or drug abuse, legal problems, domestic violence, or unemployment. If you could look behind the doors of every house on your block, you would see that every family has struggles. Some kids try to deny that problems exist by staying away from home as much as possible and by not talking honestly about the difficulties. Other kids try to fix the family problems, only to feel discouraged and frustrated by their inability to do so. Some kids are very open about family troubles, while others feel embarrassed and try to keep the problem a secret.

In your family, your parent's PTSD may be causing some special challenges. Instead of ignoring the problem or trying to fix it, you have taken a big step by reading this book, learning about PTSD, and figuring out how to deal with the situation. Good for you!

Complete the following sentences:

- ❑ Other kids often don't understand my family. It hurts when they...

- ❑ I know that my friends' parents come to their baseball games, cheerleading competitions, and school activities. When my parents cannot come to my ____________________ (fill in your activity), I feel...

- ❑ I'd really like some of my friends to be able to come over to the house, but...

Sometimes other kids may say unkind things about your parent, which can hurt a lot. For example, kids may have said that your parent is "crazy" or a "freak." Has anyone ever said something mean to you about your parent? If so, what?

How did you feel?

What did you do?

It is difficult to know what to tell your friends. You may feel confused and embarrassed about your parent's situation and believe none of your friends really understand. Or maybe you have found a couple of good friends who listen and try hard to understand.

What have you told your friends about your parent?

How have your friends responded?

How did their reactions make you feel?

When it comes right down to it, YOU are in charge of who you tell and what you tell them. That is totally your decision. For example, you may choose to ignore the kids who are rude and mean. You may be more open with some closer friends—but again, it's totally YOUR choice. You may decide to share a little bit, see how your friend responds, and then decide if you want to tell any more. You may want to tell your best friend(s) a lot more than you tell your not-so-close friends.

"Half of my friends still don't
know about my dad...
I'm pretty open about it now if someone asks...
My attitude now is:
'Yeah, my dad is sick – get over it!'
It took a lot of years to get here."

—A teenage girl

In making these decisions about what to say and to whom, you may want to create a Pros and Cons list. Let's consider how Nikki handled this issue:

Nikki's dad is a history teacher at her high school. He developed PTSD after someone came into his classroom and shot several students. Some days her dad acts just like the other dads, but other times he gets really quiet, refuses to go to work, and explodes in anger for no real reason. Nikki feels embarrassed at his behavior when her friends visit her house. To help make her decision about what to tell her close friends, Nikki made the following chart:

Pros of Telling My Friends	Cons of Telling My Friends
They'd understand why my dad acts differently	They may not understand
I could talk to them more about it	They may think my dad is weird
They'd understand why my dad doesn't always attend my school events	They may leave me out and treat me differently
Maybe my friends could be supportive and help me	They might gossip and spread rumors
They might know someone else who has PTSD	Their parents may not let them come to my house or do things with me
I wouldn't have to hide the secret any longer	I'd feel nervous about telling them

What would be the Pros and Cons in your situation? Fill in the table with your hopes and fears about sharing:

Pros of Telling My Friends	Cons of Telling My Friends

In addition to deciding IF you want to open up to your friends, it's helpful to think about WHAT to tell them. Your friends have probably heard about PTSD, but they have no idea what it's like to live with it. Society is becoming more aware and less judgmental of people with emotional problems, but we've still got a ways to go. You may decide to share with friends some of what you've learned in this book or other things you have discovered. If you're not sure what to say, here are a few helpful hints:

- PTSD is actually common. One in seven families has a parent with PTSD. My family is not alone.
- My parent goes to counseling and gets help. I'm proud of my mom or dad for trying to recover from the really awful event and for working to move on with life.

- My parent has good days and bad days. Sometimes it's hard to know what kind of a day it will be.
- Scientists have discovered many treatments that help trauma survivors to feel better.

Activity

If you could pick one thing you'd like the world to understand about PTSD, what would it be?

Create a slogan that would help people understand PTSD.

Design a banner or billboard below:

CHAPTER ELEVEN

What can I do to help?
Tips on supporting my parent

In working with families, we've learned that every teen has a unique reaction to his/her parent's situation. Before we look at your specific reaction and how you can help, it's important to remember what is working well in your relationship with your mom or dad. Your parent probably has many great qualities, and you know that PTSD does not totally define your parent. So, let's think about what you enjoy in your relationship with your parent.

Complete the following sentences:

- ❑ One of my favorite things to do with my parent is...

- ❑ Even though my parent has PTSD, I know I can count on him/her to...

- ❑ A favorite memory of a special time with my parent is...

- [ ] I'm very proud of my parent because...

When a parent has experienced trauma, most people in the family are affected to some degree. That's normal. Some young people are able to make the best of the situation and carry on somewhat as usual. Unfortunately, not all kids manage to do that; they may respond to PTSD in the family in the following ways:

- Some kids feel so badly about their parent's situation that they spend all their free time at home.

  Anna stopped going to the mall with her friends and quit the swim team. In fact, her life now revolves completely around her mom. Anna has a hard time concentrating on her homework and has even started having nightmares herself. Anna feels nervous a lot of the time.

  If Anna's behavior sounds like you, **Lesson 7** is just for you: It's very important that you take good care of yourself and have your own fun activities.

- Other kids think that if they behave really well, all the problems will go away. They blame themselves for upsetting their parent.

  Tom blames himself for his dad's anxiety and frequently tries to cheer up his dad, only to feel guilty when unsuccessful. Tom feels responsible for his dad's happiness and works very hard to make things better.

  If you're like Tom, **Lesson 8** will be important for you: Although there are many ways in which you can support your parent, you cannot make your parent's difficulties go away.

- Some families are so focused on the trauma survivor that the kids are forgotten or left out.

  Kim spends most of her time at her friends' houses because she doesn't think that her parents care about her. When Kim is at home, she is usually in her room with the door closed, and she doesn't want to talk to anyone. She feels cut off from her family and doesn't know who can really understand her.

  If you see yourself in Kim's behavior, please check out **Chapter 9**, as it helps you find people who will listen to your story and support you.

Do you see yourself in any of these reactions?

If yes, what do you see yourself doing?

How is that working for you?

Regardless of how you have responded to your parent's problems, it's clear that your relationship with your parent is not the same as it would be if he/she didn't have PTSD. Sometimes that's tough on everybody. Having a parent develop PTSD can be a real loss. Recognizing it as a loss can be a step toward greater understanding and peace for you. It can also free you from trying hard to make your parent into someone he/she is not.

Complete the following sentences:

❑ Something I miss that my parent and I don't do together anymore is...

❑ Because my parent has PTSD, I know he/she may never be able to...

Although you cannot make your parent's difficulties disappear, there are many things you can do to help. You may really want to help your parent feel better, but you aren't sure what to do.

Lesson Number 8

You can support your parent in many special ways.

How do you show your parent that you care about him/her?

What specific things do you do?

> Great opportunities to help others seldom come…
> but small ones surround us every day.
> —Sally Koch

Here are some ideas other kids developed that work for them. **Circle** any of the following that you have done, and **put a star by three** that you'd like to try. Not every idea will fit your relationship with your parent, but consider these options:

Vacuum the carpet

Do the dishes

Send your parent a kind e-mail

Walk the dog

Mow the yard

Offer to babysit your younger siblings

Rent your parent's favorite movie

Make your parent a special card

Tell your parent you love him/her

Talk with your parent about neat memories

Take out the trash

Give your parent a hug

Pick or buy flowers for your parent

Clean up your room without being asked

Fold the laundry

Look through old family scrapbooks with your parent

Talk about fun family vacations

Tell your parent that you are proud of him/her

Play cards or board games with your parent

Wash your parent's car

Make coupons to do special things for your parent

Helpful Hint:

Since you're not a mind reader, you may want to ask your parent what would be helpful to him/her.

Your parent will appreciate you for asking...and you just might learn something!

Finally, we all need quiet time by ourselves. Your parent may just need some time alone. One way you can show that you care is to give your parent space. Doing that can be tough, but your parent will probably appreciate it...even if he/she does not tell you so.

NOTE:

Although it's great to support your parent, remember: It's not your job to be the caregiver. You don't have to do anything. You may find helpful ways to support your parent, but always remember to take time for yourself, too.

"Forever I wanted to take
on the burdens of my family...
I finally learned I didn't have to do that.
The faster you can figure that out, the better."

—A teenage girl

Please use these pages for any additional thoughts and feelings that surface as you use this book.

You may wish to answer some of the questions more than once.

You may decide to draw something or write poetry to describe your feelings.

Whatever you decide, this space is for you.

PART III: Wrap-Up

- Final Thoughts and Lessons Learned
- Commonly Asked Questions
- Resource List

CHAPTER TWELVE

Final Thoughts and Lessons Learned

Congratulations on having gotten through this book!

We hope that reading and writing about your family's experiences have been interesting and helpful. We know that thinking about these problems can be difficult, so we're proud of you for hanging in there. Sometimes you probably thought about throwing this book under your bed and never opening it again...but, if you got to this page, you have obviously picked it up again. Good for you! Facing all this stuff directly takes courage.

We hope that you use the ideas and skills you have learned in this book. We trust that you now understand your parent's difficulties a bit better. You may want to come back to certain chapters later, as your thoughts and feelings will probably change over time. Some sections that don't seem to apply now may be helpful later.

You may remember that Chapter 6 talked about ways in which your parent may have grown and gotten stronger by having lived through a trauma. Researchers are learning more every day about how some trauma survivors get a more positive, hopeful outlook and re-evaluate their priorities in life.

We also hope that **you** grow as you deal with these challenges in your family. You have directly faced and dealt with some pretty serious matters. You likely learned some things about yourself. Take a minute to think about this…

What have you learned about **yourself** by going through this?

For example, some kids learn that:

- I am a really good listener.
- It's important to keep up with my schoolwork and fun activities, even when my parent is having a rough time.
- Even when my feelings seem out of control, I know I will be OK. I have a lot of things I can do to help myself feel better.
- I am good at cheering up my parent on bad days.
- I am pretty strong. I can handle a lot.
- Even though I cannot fix the problems in my family, I can love and support my parents and siblings a lot.
- There are a lot of people who care about me and will listen if I need to talk.
- Praying and reading inspirational books help me feel peaceful and close to God.

I have learned ____

____

____

____

What have you learned about **your family?**

For example, some kids learn that:

- My family really comes together when times are rough.
- I appreciate how my aunt and grandpa step in to help when my parent is having a bad time.
- I am thankful for the fun times I have with my family.

- My family really isn't that different from my friends' families. Although my family is dealing with PTSD, all families have their own problems!

I have learned ______________________________

____

____

____

We know that you probably have more questions, and we encourage you to talk to trusted adults and seek out resources (see Chapter 14) to find answers. However, remember that some questions don't have easy answers, so your challenge may be to find a way to be OK with not understanding everything. We know this is tough to do—it's tough for adults, too!

Remember: All families have problems. You have shown a lot of strength in facing your family's challenges head-on and learning as much as you can.

We hope that you practice the lessons you've learned in this book, remembering that

You Are Not Alone...

and

You Can Make It Through!

LESSONS LEARNED

1. **You are not alone!**
   PTSD is common. Actually, 1 in 7 families has a parent who has or will develop PTSD. Many more families have loved ones dealing with trauma-related stress.

2. **If your parent is distant, it is NOT because he/she doesn't love you. Your parent may be overwhelmed by strong feelings and bad memories.**
   Sometimes trauma survivors isolate themselves from other people because the memories and feelings take up a lot of energy. Kids may feel confused and hurt when their parents are zoned out and emotionally distant. It's important to remember that your parent still cares about you, but he/she is having a hard time showing it right now.

3. **People with PTSD can't "get over it" just like that.**
   Just as you would never tell someone with cancer to just "get over it," this advice makes no sense to someone who has experienced a traumatic event. The survivor would probably love to forget about the event and return to a "normal" life, but sometimes the memories are too painful. Treatment can help the survivor cope with the memories, enjoy close relationships, and lead a happy, productive life.

4. **A lot of help is available for your parent.**
   Your parent can get a lot of help from mental health professionals, but it's important for him/her to stick with treatment. There are no cures or quick fixes, but therapy and sometimes medications can be very helpful.

5. **Family support is important.**
   Each person in the family is affected when a family member has PTSD. Help is available for the entire family. Family participation in treatment can mean a lot to the trauma survivor.

6. **It's normal to have a wide range of feelings about your family.**
   Some days you may feel great about how things are going. Other days, though, you may feel worried, sad, angry, or confused. Just as PTSD can have its ups and downs, living with someone with PTSD can be a rocky road, too.

7. **Remember to take good care of yourself and have your own activities.**
   Living with a trauma survivor can be tough, so taking time to do fun things is important. Reserving time just for you is especially important when your parent is having a rough time (such as being admitted to the hospital, being really mean, or drinking a lot of alcohol). Remember that talking to a mental health professional may help you, too. Please find people to support you through the tough times.

8. **You can support your parent in many special ways.**
   No matter how hard you try, you cannot make your parent's problems disappear. However, there are many things you can do to show your mom or dad that you care.

CHAPTER THIRTEEN

Commonly Asked Questions

We hope we have answered many of your questions in this book. Below we list a few additional questions and answers that may be helpful. If you have other questions, please talk to a trusted adult, perhaps someone you identified in Chapter 9.

What is PTSD?

Post-traumatic stress disorder (PTSD) is a condition in which a person has experienced a traumatic event and has long-standing problems afterwards. The three categories of PTSD symptoms include:

- Re-living the trauma
  - Nightmares and intrusive thoughts
  - Feeling upset by reminders of the event
  - Flashbacks
- Avoiding reminders of the trauma
  - Avoiding places, people, and activities that remind the person of the trauma
  - Losing interest in activities
  - Shutting down emotionally and feeling distant from others
- Feeling tense and on edge much of the time
  - Sleep difficulties
  - Angry outbursts
  - A need to be very sure of one's surroundings

Check out Chapter 2 for more details.

Will my parent's PTSD go away?

This is a very important, but tough question. The answer probably depends on your parent's particular situation. Some people with PTSD experience some problems for their entire lives; however, they may improve dramatically and do well for long periods of time. As with other diseases such as cancer, diabetes, and asthma, scientists are working hard to develop effective treatments. Medications and therapies can make a major difference in your parent's well being. Refer back to Chapter 6 for more details on the many treatments for PTSD.

Will I get PTSD because my parent has it?

No! Your risk for developing PTSD is no greater than anyone else's risk.

What does my parent do in counseling?

Counseling provides your parent a chance to share thoughts, feelings, and experiences. People often feel a lot better after talking about their worries, sadness, and confusion. Therapists are trained to be excellent listeners, so your parent gets their undivided attention—no interruptions of cell phones or pagers. Therapists are caring, supportive people who don't judge your parent for his/her actions. Rather, therapists encourage people to make healthy choices and help them to cope better with problems.

What should I tell my friends about my family?

You decide who you want to talk to about your family situation **and** what you wish to tell them. It's totally YOUR choice. You may decide to be quite open about your parent's situation and talk freely, or you may choose to tell only a few people. Making the decisions about sharing with people can be tricky, so you may want to review the Pros and Cons chart in Chapter 10

What should I do when my friends tease me about my parent?

Being teased never feels good, but it can really hurt when someone makes fun of your parent. When this happens, you may feel many different emotions: embarrassed, hurt, sad, confused, and angry. Words can really sting, can't they?

If someone says unkind things about your parent, you may want to just walk away. You may feel like crying or just want to be by yourself. You may feel like saying something mean back, but we hope you can take the high road and walk away. When you have some space, you may tell a trusted adult, write in this book, or do something else to help yourself feel better.

If the person is really a good friend, you may decide to tell them later that their words hurt. You could teach your friend a little about PTSD in the hopes that he/she will not tease you again. However, if someone teases you a lot, that person is probably not a friend at all. You may want to steer clear of that person altogether.

What should I do if I feel in danger?

Most people with PTSD are no more dangerous than anyone else. However, if you ever feel in danger, remove yourself from the situation immediately and find a trusted adult to help. If needed, call 911 using your cell phone or a neighbor's phone.

What should I do if I start to feel depressed?

First of all, realize that going through times of feeling sad and down is normal. Almost all teenagers experience periods of feeling depressed. Having tough times does not mean that you have a serious mental illness. We hope that you review the coping skills discussed in Part Two of this book and use them to help you through the rough spots. Talking to a trusted adult can be very helpful, so we encourage you to let someone know how you feel.

If your sadness feels really intense, lasts a long time, or affects your ability to do your schoolwork, please talk to someone right away. You don't have to feel this awful. Living with PTSD in the family can be stressful, so it's understandable that you may be struggling. Check out that support system map you made in Chapter 9. You may want to talk to your parent, another relative, a school counselor, a neighbor, your family doctor, or a minister.

Sometimes depression can include thoughts of wanting to escape the sadness by dying. People may think about ways to hurt themselves to stop the pain. If you have these thoughts, please tell an adult **immediately**. If no one is around, call the 24-hour hotline (1-800-SUICIDE) or check the suicide website (www.suicidehotlines.com). Treatment for depression can be very helpful and you won't always feel this badly. Thinking about hurting yourself is very serious, so please find someone you can talk to about your thoughts and feelings.

What should I do if I have gone through a traumatic experience myself? Or, if I wonder if I have PTSD, too?

If you have experienced a traumatic event, you may have related to many of the problems and feelings that we described in this book. As we shared earlier, most people who experience a trauma end up being fine and move on with their lives. Many people use healthy coping skills and aren't bothered by the event years later. So, just having lived through a bad event doesn't mean that you will develop problems or have PTSD.

If you are having a hard time, we strongly encourage you to ask for help. Check back to the support network you created in Chapter 9 to see who can assist you in getting help. You may choose to talk to a friend or minister, or you may want to see a mental health professional. Acknowledging that you're going through a rough time and asking for help take a lot of courage. We hope you will take this important step toward feeling more in control of your feelings and your life.

CHAPTER FOURTEEN

Resource List

As promised, this chapter lists helpful resources. The first section provides information about PTSD specifically, while the rest of the chapter focuses on related issues. Each section contains recommended websites and books. Some of the books are written for adults, and a few are for young children (these may be helpful if you have younger brothers or sisters). You'll notice that there aren't many books specifically for teenagers—that's why we wrote this book for you!

Post-Traumatic Stress Disorder (PTSD)

Websites

www.ncptsd.org
National Center for Post-Traumatic Stress Disorder

www.patiencepress.com
Patience Press, including copies of the "Post-Traumatic Gazette"

www.sidran.org
Sidran Traumatic Stress Foundation

www.trauma-pages.com
David Baldwin's Trauma Information Pages

www.adaa.org
Anxiety Disorders Association of America

Books

For Adults

Trust after trauma: A guide to relationships for survivors and those who love them. (1998). A. Matsakis. Oakland, CA: New Harbinger.

Post-trauma stress. (2000). F. Parkinson. Tucson, AZ: Fisher Publishing.

For Young Children

Why is Daddy like he is? A book for kids about PTSD. (1994). P. Mason. High Springs, FL: Patience Press.

Why is Mommy like she is? A book for kids about PTSD. (1994). P. Mason. High Springs, FL: Patience Press.

December stillness. (1988). M. Hahn. Boston, MA: Clarion Books.

Depression

Websites

www.depression.org

Information about depression

www.dbsalliance.org

Depression and Bipolar Support Alliance

www.nimh.nih.gov/publicat/depression.cfm

National Institute of Mental Health

www.narsad.org/dc

National Alliance for Research on Schizophrenia and Depression

Books

For Adults

Understanding depression: What we know and what you can do about it. (2002). J. R. DePaulo and L. A. Horvitz. New York, NY: John Wiley & Sons.

What to do when someone you love is depressed. (1998). S. and M. Golant. New York, NY: Henry Holt & Co.

For Young Children

Why are you so sad? A child's book about parental depression. (2002). B. Andrews. New York, NY: Magination Press.

Bart speaks out: Breaking the silence on suicide. (1998). L. Goldman. Los Angeles, CA: Western Psychological Services.

Sad days, glad days. (1995). D. Hamilton. New York, NY: Albert Whitman Publishers.

Mommy stayed in bed this morning. (2002). M. W. Wenger. Scottdale, PA: Herald Press.

Phone Number

Depression and Bipolar Support Alliance 1-800-826-3632

Anxiety Disorders

Websites

www.adaa.org

Anxiety Disorders Association of America

www.freedomfromfear.org

Freedom From Fear

www.nimh.nih.gov/healthinformation/anxietymenu.cfm

National Institute for Mental Health

Books

For Adults

Mastery of your anxiety and panic (MAP-3): Client workbook for anxiety and panic. (2005). D.H. Barlow and M.G. Craske. New York, NY: Oxford University Press.

The anxiety and phobia workbook. 4th ed. (2005). E. J. Bourne. Oakland, CA: New Harbinger.

The sky is falling: Understanding and coping with phobias, panic, and obsessive-compulsive disorders. (1996). R. Dumont. New York, NY: W.W. Norton & Co.

Substance Abuse

Websites

www.alcoholics-anonymous.org

Online Recovery AA Resources

www.al-anon.alateen.org

Al-Anon Family Group Headquarters

www.samhsa.gov

Substance Abuse and Mental Health Services Administration

www.niaaa.nih.gov

National Institute on Alcohol Abuse and Alcoholism

Books

For Adults

How Al-Anon works for families and friends of alcoholics. (1995). Virginia Beach, VA: Al-Anon Family Groups.

Getting them sober. 3rd ed. (1998). T. R. Drews. Baltimore, MD: Recovery Communications, Inc.

For Young Children

Daddy doesn't have to be a giant anymore. (1996). J. Thomas. Boston, MA: Clarion Books.

My Dad loves me, my Dad has a disease: A child's view: Living with addiction. (1997). C. Black. Denver, CO: MAC Publishing.

Phone Number

Al-Anon (or Alateen) Meeting Information
1-888-425-2666 (888-4AL-ANON)

Mental Illness in General

Websites

www.mentalhealth.com
Encyclopedia of mental health information

www.mentalhelp.net
Includes interactive tests, support groups, and articles on various disorders

www.nami.org
National Alliance for the Mentally Ill or 1-800-950-NAMI

www.nmha.org
National Mental Health Association or 1-800-969-NMHA

www.psych.org
American Psychiatric Association

www.apa.org
American Psychological Association

www.allmentalhealth.samhsa.gov
Substance Abuse and Mental Health Services Administration

www.psychologyinfo.com/problems
Psychology Information Online

http://home.vicnet.net.au/~nnaami/

National Network of Adult and Adolescent Children who have a Mentally Ill Parent/s. Victoria, Australia

Books

For Adults

Stop pretending: What happened when my big sister went crazy. (1999). S. Sones. New York, NY: HarperCollins.

When someone you love has a mental illness: A handbook for family, friends, and caregivers. (2003). R. Woolis. New York, NY: Penguin Group USA.

For Young Children

Sometimes my mommy gets angry. (2003). B.M. Campbell and E.B. Lewis. New York, NY: Putnam.

Wish upon a star: A story for children with a parent who is mentally ill. (1991). P. Laskin and A. Moskowitz. New York, NY: American Psychological Association.

NOTE:

Remember: If anyone is in danger, go to a safe place and call 911.

National Suicide Hotline

1-800-SUICIDE (784-2433)

Suicide websites:

www.suicidehotlines.com
www.suicidecrisiscenter.com
www.suicide-helplines.org
(Suicide Helplines Around the World)

List of Feelings

afraid
alone
angry
annoyed
anxious
ashamed
blown off
bored
brave
calm
cheerful
compassionate
confident
confused
crabby
criticized
curious
dazed
depressed
disappointed
discouraged
disgusted
disrespected
embarrassed
empty
forgotten
frustrated
furious
guilty
happy
helpless
hopeful
hopeless
hurt
impatient
insecure
jealous
judged
left out
lonely
lost
loved
mad
numb
overwhelmed
powerless
panicky
proud
resentful
sad
safe
scared
strong
surprised
suspicious
tender
tense
thankful
torn
trapped
unappreciated
understanding
upset
weird
worried
worthless

Glossary

The chapter listed at the end of each definition indicates where the term is fully explained.

Addiction. A pattern of behavior in which the person is obsessed with getting something specific (such as alcohol) and often goes to great extremes to get it (Chapter 5).

Anxiety. A state of feeling worried, afraid, or keyed up, often about something bad that may happen in the future (Chapters 2 and 4).

Avoidance. A pattern of staying away from something that is scary or upsetting. The second category of PTSD symptoms involves avoiding reminders of the trauma (Chapter 2).

Coping strategies. Tools, such as deep breathing and relaxation, used to cope with strong feelings (Chapter 8).

Disorder (or mental disorder). A broad term for problems with thoughts, feelings, and behavior. The problems cause distress for the person and interfere with daily life (Chapter 1).

Emotions. Another word for feelings (Chapter 7).

Flashback. A rare experience when the person feels like the traumatic event is happening all over again (Chapter 2).

Insomnia. A long-standing difficulty with falling or staying asleep (Chapter 2).

Major depression. A condition in which the person feels sad or irritable, hopeless, guilty, uninterested in fun activities, and tired for an extended period of time (Chapter 4).

Panic attack (or anxiety attack). A frightening experience in which a person may feel very scared, wonder if he/she is dying, be short of breath, and have a racing heartbeat (Chapter 4).

Psychiatrist. A medical doctor (M.D.) who has expertise in brain functioning and who prescribes medications to help people feel better (Chapter 6).

Psychologist. A provider with a doctoral degree (Ph.D. or Psy.D.) who provides counseling, does testing, and performs research (Chapter 6).

PTSD (Post-Traumatic Stress Disorder). A condition in which a person who has experienced a traumatic event re-lives the upsetting experience, avoids reminders of the event, feels tense and on edge, and often has strong emotions (Chapters 1 and 2).

Re-experiencing. A category of PTSD symptoms in which the person relives the trauma through nightmares, intrusive thoughts, or flashbacks (Chapter 2).

Social anxiety (or social phobia). A condition in which the person feels nervous in public situations, such as giving a speech or eating at a restaurant, where he/she may be evaluated or judged (Chapter 4).

Symptom. A specific problem that a person is experiencing, such as having a hard time concentrating (Chapter 2).

Trauma. An event that involves a death, a life-threatening experience, or a serious injury (Chapter 1).

Treatment (or treatment plan). A general term for the mental health services provided to the person. Each person has a treatment plan that includes specific goals and means of helping the person reach the goals (such as counseling and medications) (Chapter 6).

Therapy (or counseling). A process in which a person meets regularly with a mental health professional to get support and to learn new ways of coping with life's difficulties (Chapter 6).

Trigger. Reminders of the trauma that are upsetting for the survivor. Triggers can be places, sounds, smells, thoughts, feelings, people, and activities (Chapter 2).

Note for Professionals

If you have this book in your hand, you obviously care about teenagers. Keeping up with the challenges teens face is a difficult task, as kids are bombarded with many complex issues at an early age. This book focuses on one important topic, namely living with a parent who has experienced trauma.

More than half of all people in the general population experience at least one traumatic event during their lifetime. Among adults receiving mental health or addiction treatment in the public health sectors, exposure to trauma is almost universal (Mueser et al., 1998; Triffleman, 1999). While approximately eight percent of people will meet criteria for PTSD at some time during their lives, many more will have problems in daily living that result from a traumatic event.

Over two-thirds of women and men with PTSD are parents, and their children need our attention. Many of these young people live every day with embarrassment, confusion, anger, guilt, and fear. The youth ask:

What is this all about and why is it happening to me?
How can I cope with my strong feelings?
What should I tell my friends?

This book addresses all of these questions as well as other aspects of understanding and coping with a traumatized parent. We strive to normalize the teen's experience, educate the teen about PTSD and other common reactions to trauma, encourage the use of healthy coping strategies, and provide resources for further learning. With a unique three-part structure, our book provides facts, practical tips, opportunities for reflection and journaling, reassurance, and most of all, hope.

We believe that this book will be useful for anyone working with teenagers and families—ranging from mental health professionals to clergy to teachers to pediatricians. We encourage you to adapt this book to fit your specific needs and clientele. Field testing has shown that the book is well suited for youth ages 11-18. However, it could be adapted to other age groups with your professional assistance. You may find the book to be helpful as bibliotherapy with teens as part of individual sessions. You may also choose to use this book as the basis for a support group for youth dealing with parental trauma. Although the chapters do build on one another, you may encourage the young person to skip around and focus on a specific topic that is most relevant to his/her needs at that time. As documented in the burgeoning literature on the physical and psychological benefits of journaling, we expect that the reader will benefit from the writing exercises scattered throughout the book. You may invite the teen to share certain sections of his/her work with you in your meetings.

We would greatly appreciate any feedback you may have about your experiences with this book, as we are committed to improving it for future readers. If you are willing to share your reactions, you can contact us through our website at ***www.seedsofhopebooks.com***.

Note for Parents/Caregivers

Living with a parent who experiences trauma-related stress or post-traumatic stress disorder (PTSD) can be tough. Oftentimes young people struggle with many questions, such as:

- What is PTSD?
- Why is my parent so angry? So depressed?
- Why can't my parent just "get over it" and go back to being normal?
- What should I tell my friends?
- How can I help my parent to feel better?

Kids react in a variety of ways to parents that have been traumatized. Since parents may be distracted by the challenges surrounding the trauma, kids sometimes grow up quickly and take on extra responsibilities. The young people may appear overly mature and confident on the outside, while feeling insecure and confused on the inside. Other kids may act out due to anger about what is happening in the family. Young people may blame themselves for the parent's struggles, thus carrying tremendous guilt inside of them.

However kids manifest their feelings, they tend to have strong, often confusing emotions. Due to the family's understandable focus on the survivor, sometimes kids' feelings are unintentionally ignored or minimized. This avoidance of the kids' feelings can heighten their sense of shame or the perception that something is very wrong.

This book deals directly with the teenager's experience and is organized into three major sections. Part One, "The Basics," covers many important facets of trauma reactions (including PTSD) such as clear definitions, stories depicting common family experiences, and discussions of treatment options. Correct and concise information is critical to living well with PTSD in the family. Part Two, "Life with a Parent Who

Has Experienced Trauma," provides a vehicle for readers to explore their feelings. This journal-like section normalizes a variety of emotional reactions your child may experience and provides opportunities for written reflection. A great deal of research has supported the healing power of journaling for both physical and mental health. We also encourage the reader to use healthy coping skills, including talking to trusted adults. Throughout the book we pose many important questions, some factual and some about feelings. We also encourage the reader to seek out additional information as needed. Please anticipate that your child may ask questions and need support. If your child confides in you, we encourage you to be open to his/her feelings and to praise your child for considering these tough issues. If you aren't able to provide support right now, assure your child that you love him/her and find someone else your child can talk to, such as a therapist, family member, or teacher. Finally, Part Three, "Wrap-Up," includes some final thoughts, a review of the eight key lessons, commonly asked questions, a resource list, a list of feelings, and a glossary.

It's important that your child feels comfortable writing his/her feelings in this book. Your child may choose to use this book as a private diary or may use the journal sections as a way of communicating with you.

We hope this book is useful for your family in coping with trauma-related stress. We believe it can educate, support, and empower your child, as well as stimulate helpful discussions among family members.

Best wishes along the journey.

Acknowledgements

Our sincere and heartfelt thank you to the many people who spent hours reviewing our book, providing incredibly helpful guidance and encouragement. This book is much stronger as a result of this community of people who has supported us along the journey. They helped our dream become a reality. Without them and their dedication, this book would still be a series of random thoughts and exercises floating around in our minds and on the computer. Each of them gave us help from a unique and honest perspective, which was truly invaluable as we fine-tuned our work. We are indebted to all of them for keeping us motivated, inspired, and driven to move forward with our passion for helping teens.

Two families allowed us the privilege of entering into their lives and hearing their stories. What they gave us cannot be measured. We will forever be grateful to them for their honesty and generosity.

Thank you to Lisa (sister/daughter) for wholeheartedly sharing our passion, for her "right on" suggestions and additions to our manuscript, and for never letting us doubt our work or lose sight of our goal.

Thank you to Dudley (father/husband) for his ever-present support, for giving us space when we needed it, for being rock-solid with his expert critique, and for his assistance with website design.

Praise and thanks to our Heavenly Father for entrusting us with this ministry. Our goal is to do His work and serve His people.

About the Authors

Michelle D. Sherman, Ph.D., is a licensed clinical psychologist and Director of the Family Mental Health Program at the Oklahoma City Veterans Affairs Medical Center. She is co-chair of the Family Studies Team of the South Central Mental Illness Research, Education and Clinical Center (MIRECC). She is also a clinical associate professor in the Department of Psychiatry and Behavioral Sciences at the University of Oklahoma Health Sciences Center. Dr. Sherman has worked extensively with families dealing with a wide range of traumatic experiences, including military combat, domestic violence, and sexual assault. She graduated from the University of Notre Dame and later earned her doctoral degree in clinical psychology from the University of Missouri at Columbia. She has published more than 25 scientific articles in professional journals, primarily focusing on family issues surrounding trauma and mental illness. She enjoys reading, exercise, movies, and spending time with her nephews, Luke and Noah.

DeAnne Sherman, Michelle's mom, is a French teacher, trained dancer, and choreographer. She graduated from the College of St. Catherine in St. Paul, Minnesota, where she received degrees in French, education, and speech and theater. She owned and operated a dance studio for ten years where she worked extensively with teens and young adults. In addition to being an experienced public speaker, DeAnne also volunteers her time teaching and mentoring junior high and high school students in the performing arts. DeAnne's mission is to educate, affirm, encourage, and cherish each of her students, whether it is in the classroom, in the dance studio, or on the stage. In her free time, she enjoys exercising, traveling, and speaking French with her grandsons.

The collaboration of psychologist and teacher, daughter and mother, brought true synergy to this project; the authors drew from and pooled their personal and professional life experiences in creating this book.

Workshops and presentations on the effects of trauma on the family are available for:

- The general public
- Mental health professionals
- Support groups
- Other professionals working with youth and families

We would be happy to customize a training program for your needs. Workshops could last one hour, a half a day, or a full day.

For more information, please see our website at:

www.seedsofhopebooks.com

Feel free to contact us via the website or at the mailing address below to discuss training options.

Seeds of Hope Books
PO Box 25737
Woodbury, MN 55125

Order Form

There are three simple ways to purchase additional copies of *Finding My Way.*

1. Order online at *www.seedsofhopebooks.com* (secure website)
2. Call BookHouse Fulfillment at 1-800-901-3480
3. Complete the form below and mail to:

   BookHouse Fulfillment, Attn: Mark Jung
   5120 Cedar Lake Road
   Minneapolis, MN 55416

Number of copies: ________________ X $20.00
Tax (6.5% MN residents only)
Shipping – one book $4.00
Shipping – additional copies ________ X $1.00
Payment Enclosed: ❑ Check or ❑ Money Order
(payable to BookHouse Fulfillment)

Shipping Address:

Name (please print): ______________________________

Address: ______________________________

City: ____________ State: ____________ Zip: ____________

Telephone: (________) ______________________________

Please call for quantity discounts.

COMING SOON:

I'M NOT ALONE:

A Teen's Guide to Living with a Parent Who Has a Mental Illness

The second in this series of Seeds of Hope Books by the daughter/mother Sherman team. This book supports teenagers whose parent has a mental illness (depression, bipolar disorder, or schizophrenia).

I'm Not Alone will be available at BookHouse Fulfillment in 2006.

Please see our website for more information: ***www.seedsofhopebooks.com***